AMERICAN EMPOWER

STUDENT'S BOOK A

WITH DIGITAL PACK

A2

ELEMENTARY

Adrian Doff, Craig Thaine
Herbert Puchta, Jeff Stranks, Peter Lewis-Jones

CAMBRIDGE

AMERICAN EMPOWER is a six-level general English course for adult and young adult learners, taking students from beginner to advanced level (CEFR A1 to C1). *American Empower* combines course content from Cambridge University Press with validated assessment from the experts at Cambridge Assessment English.

American Empower's unique mix of engaging classroom materials and reliable assessment enables learners to make consistent and measurable progress.

Content you'll love.
Assessment you
can trust.

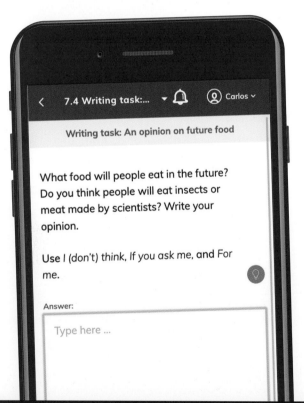

7.4 Writing task:...   Carlos

Writing task: An opinion on future food

What food will people eat in the future? Do you think people will eat insects or meat made by scientists? Write your opinion.

Use I (don't) think, If you ask me, and For me.

Answer:

Type here ...

CAN DO OBJECTIVES
- Talk about jobs
- Talk about study habits
- Ask for things and reply
- Complete a form

WORK AND STUDY

UNIT **2**

GETTING STARTED

a Look at the picture and answer the questions.
1 Where do you think the woman is?
2 What is she holding?
3 What's one good thing about her job and one bad thing?

b What kind of work do you think is interesting? Here are some ideas:
- working with people
- working with animals
- working with machines
- working on your own

19

Better Learning with *American Empower*

Better Learning is our simple approach where **insights** we've gained from research have helped shape **content** that drives **results** .

Learner engagement

1 Content that informs and motivates

Insights
Sustained motivation is key to successful language learning and skills development.

Content
Clear learning goals, thought-provoking images, texts, and speaking activities, plus video content to arouse curiosity.

Results
Content that surprises, entertains, and provokes an emotional response, helping teachers to deliver motivating and memorable lessons.

2 Personalized and relevant

Insights
Language learners benefit from frequent opportunities to personalize their responses.

Content
Personalization tasks in every unit make the target language more meaningful to the individual learner.

Results
Personal responses make learning more memorable and inclusive, with all students participating in spontaneous spoken interaction.

> *There are so many adjectives to describe such a wonderful series, but in my opinion it's very reliable, practical, and modern.*
>
> **Zenaide Brianez, Director of Studies, Instituto da Língua Inglesa, Brazil**

Measurable progress

1 Assessment you can trust

Insights
Tests developed and validated by Cambridge Assessment English, the world leaders in language assessment, to ensure they are accurate and meaningful.

Content
End-of-unit tests, mid- and end-of-course competency tests, and personalized CEFR test report forms provide reliable information on progress with language skills.

Results
Teachers can see learners' progress at a glance, and learners can see measurable progress, which leads to greater motivation.

Results of an impact study showing % improvement of Reading levels, based on global *Empower* students' scores over one year.

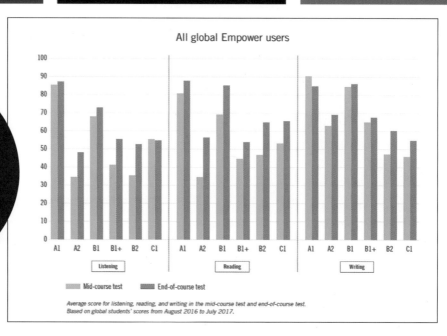

All global Empower users

Mid-course test   End-of-course test

Average score for listening, reading, and writing in the mid-course test and end-of-course test. Based on global students' scores from August 2016 to July 2017.

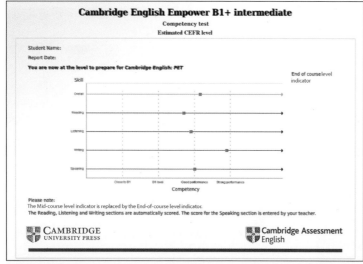

> We started using the tests provided with Empower and our students started showing better results from this point until now.

Kristina Ivanova, Director of Foreign Language Training Centre, ITMO University, Saint Petersburg, Russia

2 Evidence of impact

Insights
Schools and colleges need to show that they are evaluating the effectiveness of their language programs.

Content
Empower (British English) impact studies have been carried out in various countries, including Russia, Brazil, Turkey, and the UK, to provide evidence of positive impact and progress.

Results
Colleges and universities have demonstrated a significant improvement in language level between the mid- and end-of-course tests, as well as a high level of teacher satisfaction with *Empower*.

Manageable learning

1 Mobile friendly

Insights
Learners expect online content to be mobile friendly but also flexible and easy to use on any digital device.

Content
American Empower provides easy access to Digital Workbook content that works on any device and includes practice activities with audio.

Results
Digital Workbook content is easy to access anywhere, and produces meaningful and actionable data so teachers can track their students' progress and adapt their lesson accordingly.

3.1 Vocabulary: ... 🔔 Ⓠ Carlos ⌄

Look at the photo and choose the correct sentence.

○ They are players.

○ They are teams.

○ They are fans.

> " *I had been studying English for 10 years before university, and I didn't succeed. But now with Empower I know my level of English has changed.* "
>
> **Nikita, *Empower* Student, ITMO University, Saint Petersburg, Russia**

2 Corpus-informed

Insights
Corpora can provide valuable information about the language items learners are able to learn successfully at each CEFR level.

Content
Two powerful resources – Cambridge Corpus and English Profile – informed the development of the *Empower* course syllabus and the writing of the materials.

Results
Learners are presented with the target language they are able to incorporate and use at the right point in their learning journey. They are not overwhelmed with unrealistic learning expectations.

Rich in practice

1 Language in use

Insights
It is essential that learners are offered frequent and manageable opportunities to practice the language they have been focusing on.

Content
Throughout the *American Empower* Student's Book, learners are offered a wide variety of practice activities, plenty of controlled practice, and frequent opportunities for communicative spoken practice.

Results
Meaningful practice makes new language more memorable and leads to more efficient progress in language acquisition.

2 Beyond the classroom

There are plenty of opportunities for personalization.

Elena Pro, Teacher, EOI de San Fernando de Henares, Spain

Insights
Progress with language learning often requires work outside of the classroom, and different teaching models require different approaches.

Content
American Empower is available with a print workbook, online practice, documentary-style videos that expose learners to real-world English, plus additional resources with extra ideas and fun activities.

Results
This choice of additional resources helps teachers to find the most effective ways to motivate their students both inside and outside the classroom.

Unit overview

Unit Opener

Getting started page – Clear learning objectives to give an immediate sense of purpose.

Lessons A and B

Grammar and Vocabulary – Input and practice of core grammar and vocabulary, plus a mix of skills.

Digital Workbook (online, mobile): Grammar and Vocabulary

Lesson C

Everyday English – Functional language in common, everyday situations.

Digital Workbook (online, mobile): Listening and Speaking

Unit Progress Test

Lesson D

Integrated Skills – Practice of all four skills, with a special emphasis on writing.

Digital Workbook (online, mobile): Reading and Writing

Review

Extra practice of grammar, vocabulary, and pronunciation. Also a "Review your progress" section for students to reflect on the unit.

Mid- / End-of-course test

Additional practice

Further practice is available for outside of the class with these components.

Digital Workbook (online, mobile)

Workbook (printed)

Components

Resources – Available on cambridgeone.org

- Audio
- Video
- Unit Progress Tests (Print)
- Unit Progress Tests (Online)
- Mid- and end-of-course assessment (Print)
- Mid- and end-of-course assessment (Online)
- Digital Workbook (Online)
- Photocopiable Grammar, Vocabulary, and Pronunciation worksheets

CONTENTS

2

Contents

This page is intentionally left blank.

This page is intentionally left blank.

WELCOME!

G Possessive adjectives; Question words; *a/an*; Regular plural forms
V Numbers; The alphabet; Colors; Classroom objects and instructions

1 FIRST CONVERSATIONS

a ▶ 00.02–00.06 Listen to five short conversations. Match them with pictures a–e.

b ▶ 00.02–00.06 Listen again. Who says these sentences? Match them with pictures a–e.

1. ☐ b ☐ Nice to meet you.
2. ☐ How are you?
3. ☐ What's your name and address?
4. ☐ How do you spell that?
5. ☐ Can we pay, please?
6. ☐ Is that your apartment?

2 SAYING HELLO

a Read Conversation 1. Put the sentences in the correct order.

☐ Hello. Nice to meet you. I'm Pedro.
☐ Hello, Pedro. Nice to meet you.
☐ Hello. I'm Tony, and this is my wife, Joanna.

▶ 00.02 Listen and check your answer.

b 💬 In pairs, say hello and say your name.

c 💬 In groups of four, say hello. Say your name and introduce your partner.

d ▶ 00.03 Read Conversation 2 and complete the sentences. Listen and check your answers.

fine   thanks   how

A Hi, Nick. ¹_____ are you?
B I'm ²_____, thanks. And you?
A I'm OK, ³_____.

e 💬 Meet other students. Have a conversation with two or three people in the class.

3 NUMBERS

a ▶ 00.04 Listen to Conversation 3. Complete the bill.

How much do they pay? $ _____

ITEM	NO.	PRICE
COFFEE	(2)	$ _____
ICE CREAM	(2)	$ _____
	Total	$ _____

THANK YOU

b ▶ 00.07 Listen and circle the numbers you hear. Then say all the numbers.

13   15   16   17   12
30   50   60   70   20

c Choose the correct answer.

25 = twenty and five / twenty-five
61 = sixty-one / one and sixty
110 = a hundred ten / a hundred and ten

d Read the numbers aloud. Then say the next three numbers.

1, 2, 3, 4, …   31, 33, 35, …
10, 20, 30, …   50, 100, 150, …
15, 25, 35, …

e

d Say these colors and spell the words.

e 💬 Write two words you know in English. Say the word and ask your partner to spell it.

f ▶ **00.05** Listen to Conversation 4 and complete the name and address.

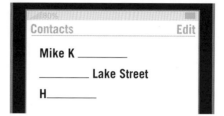

Contacts   Edit

Mike K _____

_____ **Lake Street**

H_____

g 💬 Work in pairs. Student A, tell Student B:
- your first and last name
- your address

Student B, ask Student A to spell their name and address. Write the information down. Then switch roles.

> How do you spell your … ?

5 POSSESSIVE ADJECTIVES

a ▶ **00.06** Read and listen to Conversation 5. <u>Underline</u> the correct answer.

A This is a nice photo. This is *my / your* wife and *his / her* brother.

B Oh, yes. Is that *our / your* apartment?

A Yes, that's *our / their* apartment in San Francisco.

B Mmm, it's very nice.

b Complete the chart.

our	their	her	his

I live here.	This is <u>my</u> apartment.
Do you live here?	Is this <u>your</u> apartment?
He lives here.	This is _____ apartment.
She lives here.	This is _____ apartment.
We live here.	This is _____ apartment.
They live here.	This is _____ apartment.

c Complete the sentences with a word from the chart in 5b.

1 This is my brother. _____ name is Jorge.
2 Jenny and Phil are old friends, and that's _____ car.
3 That's a good photo of you. And is that _____ daughter?
4 In this photo, we're on vacation with _____ friends Sue and Bill.
5 I know that girl in the photo. What's _____ name?

4 THE ALPHABET

a ▶ **00.08** Listen to the letters of the alphabet and say them.

A B C D E F G
H I J K L M N
O P Q R S T U
V W X Y Z

b **Pronunciation** Which letters have … ?

1 the same long sound as s**ee** /i/
2 the same long sound as d**ay** /eɪ/
3 the same short sound as **e**gg /ɛ/

c 💬 Test a partner. Student A, point to a letter. Student B, say the letter.

6 CLASSROOM OBJECTS

a Match objects 1–10 with a–j in the picture.

1 a <u>no</u>tebook	6 a <u>cup</u>board
2 a <u>dic</u>tionary	7 a desk
3 a pro<u>jec</u>tor	8 a <u>white</u>board
4 a <u>ques</u>tion	9 an <u>ans</u>wer
5 a pen	10 a <u>text</u>book

b ▶00.09 **Pronunciation** Notice the stressed syllable in the words in 6a. Listen, then practice saying the words.

c When do we usually use *an*? Choose the correct answer.
a before *a, e, i, o, u*   b before other letters

d Write *a* or *an* next to each word.

① _____ book
② _____ apple
③ _____ camera
④ _____ glass
⑤ _____ egg
⑥ _____ baby
⑦ _____ box
⑧ _____ ice cream cone

e Choose one of the words from 6a or 6d. Other students ask questions to guess the word.

Is it big? No. Is it white? No.

f Look at how words change in the plural. Complete the rules.

Singular → Plural	Rule
a pen → pens	Most words add _____ in the plural.
a baby → babies	Change a final *-y* to _____ and add _____.
a glass → glasses	If a word ends in *-s, -x, -sh,* or *-ch,* we add _____.

7 CLASSROOM INSTRUCTIONS

a ▶00.10 Listen and follow the instructions you hear. Then listen again. Which verbs do you hear each time?

open   close   look at   read   turn to   write   ask   work

b ▶00.11 <u>Underline</u> the correct words. Listen and check.

1 *What's / Who's* this? An apple or an orange?
2 *When's / Where's* Tokyo?
3 *How / What* do you say this word?
4 *Who's / When's* the president?
5 *When's / What's* your English lesson?

c Match questions 1–4 with answers a–d.

1 What's "amigo" in English?   a It's a bag you wear on your back.
2 How do you spell "night"?   b "Duh-bl."
3 What's a "backpack"?   c Friend.
4 How do you say this word?   d N-I-G-H-T.

d Write a question like questions 1–4 in 7c. Then ask other students your question.

🔄 **CAN DO OBJECTIVES**

- Talk about where you're from
- Talk about people you know
- Ask for and give information
- Write an online profile

UNIT 1

PEOPLE

GETTING STARTED

a 💬 Look at the picture and answer the questions.

1 What different countries are the people from?
2 Why are they together?
- for a sports game
- for a party
- for a music concert
3 How do they feel? Here are some ideas:

  a bored   c good   e sad
  b excited   d happy   f tired

b 💬 When do you meet people from other countries? Here are some more ideas:

- on vacation
- in a language class
- never
- at work
- at parties

1A | I'M FROM FRANCE

Learn to talk about where you're from

G *be*: affirmative and negative
V Countries and nationalities

1 LISTENING AND READING

a 💬 Look at pictures a–f and answer the questions.

1 What sport do all the people like?
2 Match countries 1–6 with pictures a–f.

1 ☐ Brazil   4 ☐ Japan
2 ☐ Spain   5 ☐ Mexico
3 ☐ Australia   6 ☐ France

b ▶️ 01.01 Listen and check. Practice saying the countries.

c ▶️ 01.02 André and Valentina are at the World Cup. Listen and check (✓) the three things they talk about.

1 ☐ soccer   4 ☐ a city
2 ☐ countries   5 ☐ TV
3 ☐ food

d ▶️ 01.02 Listen again. Complete the conversation.

ANDRÉ Hi there! My name's André. What's your ¹_____?
VALENTINA I'm Valentina.
ANDRÉ Hi, Valentina! Where are you ²_____? Colombia?
VALENTINA Yeah, you're right! I'm Colombian. I'm from Cartagena.
ANDRÉ Oh, yes! It's a really beautiful city.
VALENTINA Yes, I think so, too. So, ³_____ are you from, André?
ANDRÉ Me? I'm from ⁴_____. I'm French.
VALENTINA Oh, the French team's really good!
ANDRÉ Of course! We're ⁵_____!

e Are sentences 1–4 true or false?

1 André and Valentina are friends.
2 Valentina is from Colombia.
3 André likes Cartagena.
4 Valentina says the soccer team from France is very bad.

f Underline the two nationalities in the conversation in 1d.

2 VOCABULARY
Countries and nationalities

a André says:

I'm from **France**. I'm **French**.

▶ **01.03** Find other pairs of countries and nationalities in the box below. Listen and check.

Co|lom|bi|a	Bra|zil|ian	Span|ish	Ja|pan
Co|lom|bi|an	Ger|many	Ja|pa|nese	Ger|man
Bra|zil	Spain		

b ▶ **01.03** **Pronunciation** Notice how many syllables each word has. <u>Underline</u> the stressed syllable in each word in the box in 2a.

c ▶ **01.03** Listen again and repeat.

d Make sentences about the people below with the words in 2a.

1 Valentina: She's <u>Colombian</u>. She's from _____.
2 The people in pictures a–f: They're _____.
They're from _____.

e 💬 Look at the conversation in 1d again. Complete the question. Then ask your partner.

_____ are you from?

I'm from _____.
I'm _____.

f ≫ Now go to Vocabulary Focus 1A on p. 162 for more countries and nationalities.

3 GRAMMAR
be: affirmative and negative

a ▶ **01.06** Listen to the next part of the conversation between André and Valentina. What do they talk about?

a their soccer teams
b the town where Andre is from

b ▶ **01.06** Underline the correct answers. Listen again and check.

1 André *'s / 's not* from Paris.
2 Valentina's friends *are / aren't* from Cartagena.
3 André and Valentina *are / aren't* in the hotel.
4 *It's / It's not* 8:00.

c Look at the pairs of sentences and complete the rules.

1 I'm from France. I'm not from Paris.
2 It's a town near Paris. It's not very big.
3 They're all in the hotel. They're not here.

> To make *am*, *is*, and *are* negative, we add _____.
> We often use contractions for the verb:
> it **is** not = it**'s** not   they **are** not = they**'re** not
> I **am** not = I**'m** not
>
> We sometimes use contractions for *not*:
> It is**n't** = it's **not**   they are**n't** = they're **not**
> But never: ~~amn't~~
>
> Her friends aren't at the game.
> Valentina's sister isn't from Medellin.

d Complete the chart with the correct forms of the verb *be*.

Affirmative (+)	Negative (−)
I'm___ from Cartagena.	I _____ French.
He _____ a really good player.	She _____ from Medellín.
They say they _____ tired.	They _____ at the game.

e ≫ Now go to Grammar Focus 1A on p. 138.

f André and Valentina talk more in the café. Add the verb *be* to make correct sentences.

André says: 1 My brother in college in Madrid.
              2 My mother and father not here.

Valentina says: 3 Cartagena very hot in August.
              4 My friends really interesting and fun.

g Write two affirmative and two negative sentences about you with the verb *be*. Make two of them false.

h 💬 Read your sentences to a partner and say if your partner's sentences are true or false.

4 SPEAKING

a ≫ **Communication 1A** Student A go to p. 130. Student B go to p. 133.

b 💬 Work in small groups. Tell other students:

- your name
- your hometown
- your country and nationality

11

1 READING

a 💬🗨 Look at pictures a–d. Where do you think the people are?

b Read the texts and match them with pictures a–d. Are your ideas in 1a correct?

c Who do you think says sentences 1–4?
1 "I have four classes every day."
2 "It's fun to travel with friends."
3 "My family members live in different places."
4 "She speaks two languages – Spanish and Portuguese."

d 💬🗨 Who would you like to meet: Suzi, James, Alex, or Saddah? Why?

Now Photo!

 Suzi

This is me in Rio de Janeiro with my friend Claudia. She lives in Brazil, but she's from Spain. She's a wonderful person – very warm and kind.

📷 view Suzi's photos   💬 leave Suzi a message

 James

In this photo I'm chatting with my cousin, Eric. He lives in San Francisco. He's American, but I'm from England – Eric's mother and my father are brother and sister. Eric is a really nice guy, and he's a great doctor. He's well known in his part of San Francisco.

📷 view James's photos   💬 leave James a message

Alex

In this photo, I'm on vacation with my friend Tom. He's a fantastic friend, and he's very cool. He's a great person to be on vacation with.

📷 view Alex's photos   💬 leave Alex a message

 Saddah

This is my coworker Maram. We're teachers, and we work together in a school. She's quiet, but she's really friendly. She's also very popular with her students.

📷 view Saddah's photos   💬 leave Saddah a message

2 VOCABULARY
Adjectives

a Look at the sentence. The <u>underlined</u> words are adjectives. Are they about Rio de Janeiro or Claudia?

She's a <u>wonderful</u> person – very <u>warm</u> and <u>kind</u>!

b <u>Underline</u> eight more adjectives in the texts. Then put them in the correct blanks.

1 very good: _____, _____,
   _____
2 nice: *warm*, _____, _____
3 famous: _____
4 he/she doesn't talk much: _____
5 people like him/her: _____

c Pronunciation Three words in the texts have the /k/ sound:

<u>k</u>ind   <u>c</u>ool   <u>q</u>uiet

<u>Underline</u> the /k/ sound in these words. Which two words do not have /k/?

cold   car   cheap   kitchen   like
coffee   quick   back   key   know
come   make   school   cat

d 💬 Talk about people you know. Use adjectives from 2b.

> My friend Emma's very friendly and very popular.

> My best friend Joe's a cool guy.

> My aunt Sophia's fantastic – she's a very warm and friendly woman.

e ⟫ Now go to Vocabulary Focus 1B on p. 163 for more adjectives.

3 LISTENING

a ▶ 01.10 Listen to the conversation. Complete the nationalities (1–3) on the profiles below.

b ▶ 01.10 Listen again. Complete the profiles with adjectives 4–6.

Name: Roman
Nationality 1_____
Personality 4_____

Names: Diego and Mia
Nationality 2_____
Personality 5_____

Name: Laura
Nationality 3_____
Personality 6_____

4 GRAMMAR *be*: questions and short answers

a ▶ 01.11 Complete the answers with the words in the box. Listen and check.

_____
're not   's not   is   are
_____

1 Is she Italian?   No, she _____. She's from Spain.
2 Is he from Poland?   Yes, he _____.
3 Are they married?   Yes, they _____.
4 Are they Brazilian?   No, they _____. They're from Mexico.

b Complete the chart with the correct forms of the verb *be*.

Questions (?)		Short answers	
Are you Australian?	Yes, I _am_.	No, I'm not.	
_____ you Brazilian?	Yes, we are.	No, we're not./we aren't.	
_____ he/she Turkish?	Yes, he/she _____.	No, he/she _____.	
_____ they Ecuadorian?	Yes, they _____.	No, they _____.	

c ⟫ Now go to Grammar Focus 1B on p. 138.

d ▶ 01.13 Complete the conversations. Use contractions *'s (not)* and *'re (not)* if possible. Listen and check.

A My friend Tony ¹ _'s_ English. He ² _____ very kind.
B ³ _____ he from London?
A Yes, he ⁴ _____.

A My friends, Joe and Mel, ⁵ _____ American. They ⁶ _____ very warm and friendly.
B ⁷ _____ they married?
A No, they ⁸ _____ not. They ⁹ _____ just good friends.

5 SPEAKING

a Write down words about friends, family, and famous people you know from other countries.

Camilla – British, cool, popular   Gabriel – Mexican, quiet, kind

b 💬 Talk about the people you know. Look at the conversations in 4d to help you.

1 LISTENING

a ▶01.14 Listen to Part 1. Choose the correct answers to complete the sentences.

1 Jenny wants to
  a see the city.   b go to the hotel.
2 Richard wants to
  a look at the water. b sleep.
3 It's after nine o'clock
  a in the morning.   b at night.

b ▶01.15 Richard and Jenny talk to the hotel receptionist. Listen to Part 2. What does Jenny want to do? Choose the correct answer.

a join a gym   c take a yoga class
b sleep

c ▶01.15 Listen to Part 2 again. Are the sentences true or false? Correct the false sentences.

1 The class starts at 6:30.
2 Jenny and Richard want to go to the yoga class.
3 The fitness center is on the third floor.

2 USEFUL LANGUAGE
Asking for and giving information

a Who says sentences 1–7 at a hotel: the receptionist (*R*) or a guest (*G*)?

1 When's the first class?   a Taylor.
2 Do you have an exercise   b You're welcome.
  room?   c T-A-Y-L-O-R.
3 How can I help you?   d It's at six thirty.
4 Thanks for your help.   e It's in the fitness center
5 Can you spell that, please?   on the second floor.
6 And where's the class?   f Hi. We're checking in.
7 What's your last name?   g We do. And yoga classes, too.

b ▶01.15 Match 1–7 with a–g. Listen to Part 2 again and check.

c Underline the correct answers.

1 It's **in** *ten after four / room 6*.
2 It's **at** *eight o'clock / the first floor*.

d ▶01.16 A is a receptionist and B wants information. Complete the conversation. Look at 2a and 2b to help you. Listen and check.

A Hello. How can I ¹_____ you?
B I'd ²_____ to take a computer class.
A No problem.
B When's the first class?
A It's tomorrow at eight o'clock.
B And ³_____ the class?
A It's in room 5.
B Great. Can I sign up for the class?
A Certainly. ⁴_____ your last name?
B Moore.
A Can you ⁵_____ that, please?
B M–O–O–R–E.
A Thank you. Enjoy the class.

e 💬 In pairs, practice the conversation in 2d. Use your own last name. Take turns being A and B.

3 LISTENING

a ▶️**01.17** Listen to Part 3. Are the sentences true or false? Correct the false sentences.

1 It's 6:30 in the morning.
2 Jenny is tired.
3 Jenny wants to see San Francisco now.
4 Richard wants to see San Francisco now.

b 💬 When do you like to exercise?

- before work / school
- at lunchtime
- after work / school
- never

4 CONVERSATION SKILLS
Checking understanding

a Complete the mini-conversations with the words in the box.

| so that's   excuse me |

SONIA It's at seven twenty.
LEO ¹_____?
SONIA 7:20.

SONIA It's on the fourth floor.
LEO ²_____ 7:20 on the fourth floor.

b Which expression in 4a means:

1 I'm not sure and I want to check.
2 I don't understand. Can you say that again?

c ▶️**01.18 Pronunciation** Listen to what Leo says in 4a. Does the intonation go up ↗ or down ↘ on 1 and 2?

d 💬 Work in pairs. Use the dialogue map to practice checking understanding. Take turns being A and B.

A   B

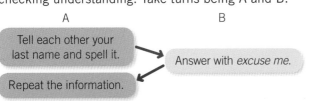

Tell each other your last name and spell it.

Answer with *excuse me*.

Repeat the information.

5 PRONUNCIATION
Consonant clusters

a ▶️**01.19** Listen to the time. Notice how the consonant clusters in **bold** are pronounced.

ei**ght** o'**cl**o**ck**
  /t/   /kl/ /k/

b ▶️**01.20** Listen to the words below. How many consonant sounds do the letters in **bold** have?

three   si**x**   ei**ght**y

c ▶️**01.21** Practice saying these times. Listen and repeat.

1 seven o'clock (7:00)   4 three forty (3:40)
2 six ten (6:10)   5 six thirty (6:30)
3 eight twenty (8:20)   6 twelve twenty (12:20)

6 SPEAKING

a ⟫ **Communication 1C** Student A go to p. 131. Student B go to p. 133.

Student A go to p. 131. Student B go to p. 133.

✔ UNIT PROGRESS TEST

→ **CHECK YOUR PROGRESS**

You can now do the Unit Progress Test.

1D | SKILLS FOR WRITING
I'm Carla and I'm from Mexico

1 SPEAKING AND LISTENING

a 💬 Ask and answer the questions.

1 Do you use a social media site?
2 Do you have an online profile?
3 Which of the following information is on it?

- your name
- your age
- your nationality
- where you live
- your job
- things you like

b Look at Kate's and Carla's profiles and complete the chart with yes (✓), no (✗), or don't know (DK).

She's ...	20 years old	from Chicago	Mexican	a teacher	a student
Kate	DK				
Carla	✓				

c ▶ 01.22 The people in the picture are in an English class. Listen and answer the questions.

1 Is this the first or the last day of the class?
2 What city are they in?

d ▶ 01.22 Listen again. Complete the chart.

Name	Country	One other thing we know
Kate and Mike	the U.S.	They're _____.
Carla	Mexico	She's a _____.
Masato		English is _____ for his work.
Carmen		She's a computer science _____ .
Orhan		His _____ is in Chicago.
Marisa		Her _____ is in Chicago.

KATE **MARKS**

💼	Teacher, International College
📅	Age: -
🌐	Lives in Chicago, the U.S.

About Kate

👥	Friends: 132 VIEW
📷	Photos VIEW

CARLA **FLORES**

💼	Student, University of Guadalajara
📅	Age: 20
🌐	Lives in Guadalajara
🌐	From Puerto Vallarta, Mexico

About Carla

👥	Friends: 189 VIEW
📷	Photos VIEW

e 💬 Work in groups of five or six. It's your first day at International College.

Student A: You're the teacher.
The others: You're one of the students in the picture.

Say who you are and say one more thing.

> I'm Martina.
> My hometown is Puebla.

16

2 READING

a Read Kate and Carla's profiles for the new class. <u>Underline</u> any new information.

I'm Kate Marks. I'm from Royal Oak. It's a small city near Detroit, Michigan, in the U.S. I live in Chicago, and I'm a teacher at International College. I'm married, and I have two young children: a boy and a girl.

I like languages, music, and movies.

< Back

I'm Carla Flores. I'm Mexican. I'm from Puerto Vallarta, but I study marketing at the University of Guadalajara. It's my first time in Chicago and I'm very happy to be here. Are other people new to Chicago?

I like running, swimming, and yoga.

< Back

3 WRITING SKILLS
Capital letters and punctuation

a Look at the profiles in 2a. Check (✓) the words that have capital letters.

1 ☐ first names of people
2 ☐ last names of people
3 ☐ names of companies, schools, universities
4 ☐ names of countries and nationalities
5 ☐ names of sports
6 ☐ names of towns or cities
7 ☐ all nouns
8 ☐ all words at the start of a sentence
9 ☐ the word *I*

b *I'm = I am.* What are the full forms of these contractions?

1 it's
2 she's
3 you're
4 isn't
5 aren't

c Correct the words. Add an apostrophe (') to each word.

1 Im
2 arent
3 isnt
4 hes
5 were
6 theyre

d Look at the commas (,) and periods (.) in the online profiles. Which do we use … ?

a at the end of a sentence
b after words in a list

e Correct the sentences. Add capital letters and punctuation (. , ' ?).

i live in paris its amazing ➜ I live in Paris. It's amazing.

1 im from shanghai its a big city in china
2 i like basketball old cars and jazz
3 im a french teacher in australia
4 this isnt my first time in miami
5 are all the teachers american

4 WRITING

a Write a profile about yourself. Use the profiles in 2a to help you. Give this information:

- your name
- your nationality
- your hometown
- your job
- what you like

b Switch profiles with another student and check the capital letters and punctuation.

Update Your Profile

Add Photo

Upload File   Take a Photo

I'm _____
_____
_____
_____
_____
_____

I like _____
_____
_____
_____
_____
_____
_____
_____

Save

UNIT 1
Review and extension

1 VOCABULARY

a Complete the sentences with the correct nationality word.

1 Vera's from Rio de Janeiro. She's _____.
2 Pedro's from Quito. He's _____.
3 Kurt and Erika are from Berlin. They're _____.
4 Ellen's from Melbourne. She's _____.
5 Claude and Sabine are from Paris. They're _____.
6 Takashi's from Tokyo. He's _____.

b Complete the text about Vera with the correct adjective.

Vera's family members are all [1]f_____c. Her mother's
[2]w_____m and [3]k_____d, and her father is very [4]n_____e.
He's a [5]g_____t doctor. Her sister Pia is [6]q_____t, but she's
very [7]f_____y.

2 GRAMMAR

a Complete the text with the correct form of the verb *be*.
Use contractions where possible.

Hi. I [1]_____ Paolo and I [2]_____ from Sydney, Australia.
I [3]_____ a college student. I [4]_____ really lucky because
I live near my sister Barbara. She [5]_____ an English teacher,
and she [6]_____ very popular with her students. She [7]_____
very kind and friendly. We [8]_____ Australian, but our parents
[9]_____ from Italy. They [10]_____ doctors.

b Write questions for the answers. Use the word in italics
to start your question.

1 *Are …?*   No, I'm not. I'm Brazilian.
2 *Is …?*   Yes, she's very kind.
3 *Are …?*   No, they aren't. They're from Germany.
4 *What's …?*   My name's Abdul Aziz.
5 *Where …?*   I'm from Venezuela.

c Write questions and short answers.

1 you Ecuadorian?   Yes
2 she your sister?   No
3 they friendly?   Yes
4 you both from the U.S.? No
5 he well known?   No

d Complete the conversation with one word in each
blank. A contraction (*I'm, you're, he's*) is one word.

A Hello. What's [1]_____ name?
B I'm Juan.
A [2]_____ you from Mexico?
B Yes, [3]_____ from Jalisco.
A And that woman over there. Is [4]_____ your sister?
B No, she [5]_____. She's a student at my school.
A OK. And [6]_____ she from?
B She's Italian. [7]_____ from Venice.

e 💬 Practice the conversation in 2d with a partner and
use your own personal information.

3 WORDPOWER *from*

a Match sentences 1–4 with pictures a–d.

1 Is the flight **from** Hong Kong here?
2 I'm not American. I'm **from** Canada.
3 The stores are open **from** 9:00 a.m. to 6:00 p.m.
4 My house is about five kilometers **from** downtown.

b Match examples 1–4 in 3a with rules a–d.

We use *from* to talk about:
a times
b a starting place
c our country or city
d how far away something is

c Match sentences 1–4 with rules a–d in 3b.

1 Our lunch break is from 12:30 to 1:30.
2 Our hotel's about five kilometers from the airport.
3 The plane from Paris is now at gate two.
4 I'm from Argentina.

d Add *from* in the correct place in these sentences.

1 This postcard is New Zealand.
2 Breakfast is seven o'clock to ten o'clock every morning.
3 The bank's only 200 meters here.

e Put the phrases in the correct order to make
sentences.

1 from / Denmark / I'm
2 open from / the supermarket's / 7:30 a.m. to 9:30 p.m.
3 my place is / from school / two kilometers

f Are the sentences in 3e true for you? Change them
to make them true.

I'm not from Denmark. I'm from Australia.

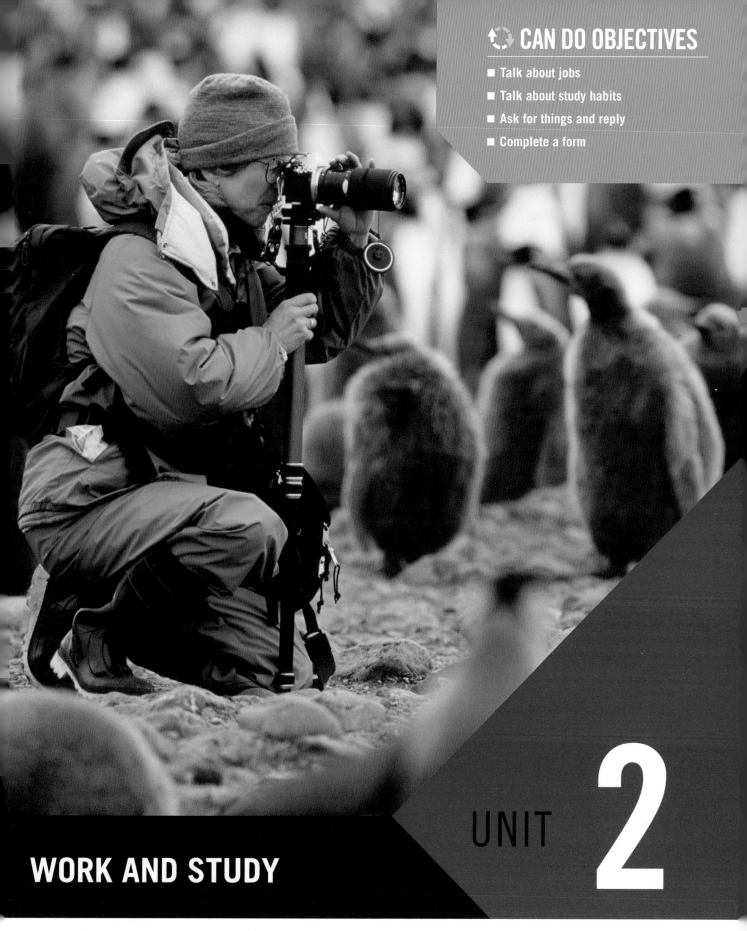

♻ **CAN DO OBJECTIVES**

■ Talk about jobs
■ Talk about study habits
■ Ask for things and reply
■ Complete a form

UNIT **2**

WORK AND STUDY

GETTING STARTED

a 💬 Look at the picture and answer the questions.

1 Where do you think the woman is?
2 What is she holding?
3 What's one good thing about her job and one bad thing?

b 💬 What kind of work do you think is interesting? Here are some ideas:

• working with people
• working with animals
• working with machines
• working on your own

1 READING

a Look at the picture. Answer the questions.

1 Where is this woman?
   a in a park   c by a river
   b at home
2 Do you think ... ?
   a she's a tourist   b she works here
3 What do you know about alligators?

b Read the article and check your answers.

c Choose the correct answers.

1 Most people *like* / *don't like* alligators.
2 Gabby Scampone *likes* / *doesn't like* alligators.
3 Alligators *like* / *don't like* people swimming near them.
4 It *is* / *is not* dangerous to give alligators food.
5 Gabby has *one job* / *two jobs*.

d Read the article again. Find two reasons why Gabby's work is interesting.

e Talk about the questions.
1 Would you like Gabby's job? Why / Why not?
2 What other unusual jobs do you know?

GATOR GIRL

Gabby Scampone with an alligator

Everglades Holiday Park is an animal park in the U.S. It's in Florida. It has birds, fish, and . . . alligators! Many tourists visit the park every year. They come to look at the alligators. Most people think alligators are interesting, but they don't really like them, and they don't go too close to them!

Gabby Scampone is different. She lives in Florida, and she works at the park. She loves her job – and she also loves alligators. In her work, she teaches visitors about alligators. She tells visitors that alligators are not always dangerous animals. Usually, alligators don't attack people, but they don't like when people swim in the water near them. Also, if people give food to alligators, sometimes the alligators get too close, and that can be dangerous.

Gabby doesn't always work at the park. She also has a second job: she catches wild alligators. If a wild alligator goes near a person's house, Gabby and some other people catch it. They take the alligators back to the park. Her parents and friends think she's crazy, but she really enjoys the job. Gabby thinks many people don't understand alligators very well, but that alligators are smart and amazing animals. And so far she still has all of her fingers!

2 VOCABULARY Jobs

a Match words 1–9 with pictures a–i.

1 ☐ nurse   4 ☐ dentist   7 ☐ janitor
2 ☐ salesperson   5 ☐ pilot   8 ☐ photographer
3 ☐ police officer   6 ☐ engineer   9 ☐ taxi driver

b ▶ **02.01** **Pronunciation** Listen to the words and underline the stressed syllable.

police officer   engineer   photographer   dentist

c 💬 Complete the sentences with jobs from 2a. Talk about your answers.

1 A(n) _____ has a dangerous job.
2 A(n) _____ has an easy job.
3 A(n) _____ has an exciting job.
4 The pay for a(n) _____ isn't very good.

d ≫ Now go to Vocabulary Focus 2A on p. 163 for more jobs vocabulary.

3 GRAMMAR
Simple present: affirmative and negative

a ▶ **02.03** Look at the sentences from 1b and complete them with the verbs from the box. Listen and check.

catches come doesn't don't (x2) go attack think work works

	I / we / you / they	*he / she / it*
+	Tourists _____ to look at the alligators. Her parents _____ she's crazy.	She _____ at Everglades Holiday Park. She _____ wild alligators.
–	They _____ too close to them. Alligators _____ people.	Gabby _____ always at the park.

b Underline more simple present verbs in the text in 1b. Make two lists: affirmative and negative forms.

c ≫ Now go to Grammar Focus 2A on p. 140.

d Underline the verbs in sentences 1–2.

1 She loves her job.
2 She catches wild alligators.

e ▶ **02.05** **Pronunciation** Which verb in 3d has an extra syllable when we add the letter -*s*? Listen and check.

f Underline the correct answers.

1 After the sounds /z/, /s/, /dʒ/ (spelled *j*), /ʃ/ (spelled *sh*), and /tʃ/ (spelled *ch*), we *don't add* / *add* an extra syllable.
2 We *don't add* / *add* an extra syllable after other sounds.

g ▶ **02.06** Listen to these verbs. Check (✓) the verbs that have an extra syllable.

☐ works   ☐ eats   ☐ teaches
☐ finishes   ☐ listens   ☐ stops
☐ catches   ☐ uses   ☐ watches

h ≫ **Communication 2A** Student A go to p. 130. Student B go to p. 133.

4 SPEAKING

a Think about your job or the job of someone you know. Write four sentences about the job: two affirmative (+) and two negative (–). Use the verbs in the box.

work drive have like study
speak go start leave know

+ I start work at 7:00 in the morning.
– I don't drive to work.

b 💬 Tell your partner your sentences. Can they guess the job?

c Tell other students about your partner's job. Can they guess it?

She starts work at …

2B | DO YOU WORRY ABOUT EXAMS?

Learn to talk about study habits
- **G** Simple present: questions and short answers
- **V** Studying; Time

1 READING

a 💬 Ask and answer the questions.

1 Are you good at taking exams?
2 Do you worry about exams and tests?
3 Do you study a lot for an exam or test?

b Read comments 1–3 in the online chat and match them with pictures a–c.

c 💬 Read the comments again and answer the questions with a partner.

1 Which study habits are … ?
   • useful   • funny
2 Put the study habits in the order you want to try them from 1 (really want to try) to 3 (don't want to try).

2 VOCABULARY Studying

a Look at the <u>underlined</u> words in questions 1–7. Match them with pictures d–j below.

1 Do you have a <u>break</u> in the middle of your English class?
2 Do you have a <u>schedule</u> for your study routine?
3 Do you take <u>notes</u> when you read something in English?
4 Do you get good <u>grades</u> in English tests?
5 How many weeks is a <u>semester</u> at your school?
6 Do you have an <u>exam</u> at the end of the year?
7 Do you <u>study</u> with your friends?

b Match the words in the box with 1–4. You can use some of the words more than once.

get	good	pass	bad	take	fail

1 an exam   3 notes
2 grades   4 a test

c 💬 Ask and answer the questions in 2a.

Exam stress!

Hi guys! I have a big exam on Friday. It's really hard to study. I read my study notes for an hour, and then I watch really bad TV shows! What about you? Do you worry about exams? What are your study habits?   **MIMI23**

1 Yeah I hate tests. They're really difficult, and I can't always remember everything. I need to study every day and take a lot of notes. It's not easy, but it helps to listen to R&B music – really loud! It helps me think.
SOUL BOY2   **REPLY** 🔗

2 I agree – exams and tests are really, really hard. In my study breaks I play with my pet cat. Some people say that animals stop stress and relax people. I think it's true, well, for me it is! Everybody needs a cat to help them study!
CAT LOVER5   **REPLY** 🔗

3 I think it helps to have a good study routine. I make a study schedule and that helps me to pass my exams. I always plan a lot of breaks and have a cup of tea and something small to eat. I don't want to get tired when I study! But the breaks are only short – about five or ten minutes. Then I go back to studying hard for one or two hours. Good grades come from a lot of hard work!
BOOKWORM8   **REPLY** 🔗

Tania and Jack

3 LISTENING

a ▶**02.07** Jack talks to Tania about her study habits. Listen and check (✓) the things they talk about.

1 ☐ places to study   3 ☐ exams
2 ☐ hours of study   4 ☐ free time

b ▶**02.07** Listen again. Complete the information about Tania's studies.

- Part-time or full-time student?
- Hours a week?
- When?
- Where?

4 VOCABULARY   Time

a Match the times that Tania talks about with the clocks.

1 Usually at **eight thirty**…
2 … last night at **a quarter after eleven**.

b Complete the sentences with the words in the box.

to   after   o'clock   thirty

1 four _____   3 (a) quarter _____ four

2 four _____   4 (a) quarter _____ five

c ≫ Now go to Vocabulary Focus 2B on p. 164 for more practice with time vocabulary.

5 GRAMMAR   Simple present: questions

a ▶**02.09** Look at the questions. Which is correct? Listen and check.

1 You a full-time student or a part-time student?
2 Are you a full-time student or a part-time student?
3 You are a full-time student or a part-time student?

b Complete the questions with one word.

_____ … you study engineering?
… they like tests?

c ▶**02.10** Jack asks Tania about her daughter, Ellie. Listen and complete the information about Ellie's studies.

- Hours a week?
- When?
- Where?

d Read the question Jack asks Tania.

Does she study more before an exam?

Look at the questions in 5b. How are they different? Why?

e ≫ Now go to Grammar Focus 2B on p. 140.

f ▶**02.12** Put the questions in the correct order. Listen and check.

1 a week / do you study / hours / how many?
2 study grammar / or vocabulary / do you?
3 you / when / study / do?
4 study / do / where / you?

g ▶**02.12** **Pronunciation** Notice the pronunciation of *do you* in each question. Can you hear both words clearly?

6 SPEAKING

a Look at the questions in 5f. Write another question about studying.

b 💬🗨 Ask and answer your questions in 6a.

c 💬🗨 Do you have any new ideas about studying now?

> Natalia studies very early in the morning because she isn't very tired. I think it's a good idea, but I prefer to sleep!

2C | EVERYDAY ENGLISH
I'd like a latte

Learn to ask for things and reply
S Reacting to news
P Sound and spelling: *ou*

1 LISTENING

a 💬 Look at the pictures. Where are Martina and Tomás?

1 at school   2 at work   3 in a coffee shop

b ▶ 02.13 Listen to Part 1 and check your answer in 1a.

c 💬 Work in pairs. Choose the correct answers.

1 Tomás orders a *small / large* coffee, a *small / large* latte, and *one muffin / two muffins*.
2 It costs *$7.25 / $8.25*.
3 Martina asks Tomás for *help / a croissant*.

d ▶ 02.13 Listen to Part 1 again and check your answers in 1c.

e ▶ 02.14 Listen to Part 2. What does Martina need help with? Choose one answer.

She asks Tomás to help her ... .
a pay for school   b study for a test   c make dinner

f ▶ 02.14 Listen to Part 2 again. Are the sentences true or false? Correct the false sentences.

1 Martina asks Tomás for help.
2 Tomás is free tonight.
3 Martina isn't free on Friday.
4 Martina's test is on Friday.

g 💬 Where do you usually meet friends and family?

• in your home
• in their home
• in a coffee shop
• in a different place

2 USEFUL LANGUAGE
Asking for things and replying

a Look at these ways to ask for things. Who says them: Tomás (*T*) or Martina (*M*)?

1 Can we have a coffee and a latte, please?
2 Could I come to your place tonight?
3 Could I have a blueberry muffin instead?
4 I need your help to get ready for a big math test.

b ▶ 02.13–02.14 Listen to Parts 1 and 2 again and check. Match a–d with 1–4 in 2a.

a So a large latte and a small coffee? Anything else?
b Oh, sure! No problem.
c Of course. It's the same price.
d Sorry, I have to work tonight.

c 💬 In pairs, take turns asking for things and replying. Use the phrases from 2a and 2b.

3 CONVERSATION SKILLS
Reacting to news

a ▶ **02.16** Complete the mini-conversations with words in the box. Listen and check your answers.

problem   bad

SAM   Sorry, I have another meeting in five minutes.
LARA   OK, no ¹_____. We can talk later.

LARA   Sorry, I have plans tonight.
SAM   Oh, that's too ²_____.

b Read the mini-conversations in 3a again. Which phrase means … ?

1 "It's not important."
2 "I'm not happy about it."

c Match a–d with 1 or 2 in 3b.

a Never mind.
b I'm sorry about that.
c It doesn't matter.
d What a shame.

4 PRONUNCIATION
Sound and spelling: *ou*

a ▶ **02.17** Listen to the sound of the letters *ou* below.

1 an online c**ou**rse
2 h**ou**se

Do the letters in 1 and 2 have different sounds?

b ▶ **02.18** Do these words sound like 1 or 2 in 4a? Listen and check. Listen again and repeat.

out __2__   four _____   your _____
about _____   sound _____

5 SPEAKING

a ⟫ **Communication 2C** Student A go to p. 130. Student B go to p. 133.

d ▶ **02.15** Listen to three short conversations. Where are they? Match them with pictures a–c.

e ▶ **02.15** Complete the sentences from the conversations in 2d. Listen again and check your answers.

1 _____ some water, please?
2 _____ a chicken sandwich, please.
3 _____ you this afternoon?

f Look at the situations. What can A and B say? Use expressions from 2a and 2b.

       A   B

1 You're in B's home. Ask for some water. → Say yes.

2 You're in a café. Ask for a small espresso. → You're the waiter. Say yes.

3 You have a problem at work. Ask for some help. → Say no. (You're busy.)

4 You want to meet B on Saturday. → Say no. (You aren't free then.)

g 💬 Work in pairs. Use the dialogue maps to ask for things and reply. Take turns being A and B.

✓ UNIT PROGRESS TEST

→ CHECK YOUR PROGRESS

You can now do the Unit Progress Test.

2D SKILLS FOR WRITING
I need English for my job

1 SPEAKING AND LISTENING

a 💬🔊 Why do you want to study English?
- to get a good job
- to study something in English
- to meet new friends
- a different reason
- for travel and tourism

b ▶️02.19 Listen to three International College students talk about where they're from and their reasons for studying English. <u>Underline</u> the correct answers.

I'm from *Acapulco / Mexico City*, and I need English for my *job / studies*.

Daniela

I'm from *Riyadh / Jeddah*, and I need English for my *job / studies*.

Said

I'm from *Tokyo / Osaka*, and I need English for my *job / studies*.

Sakura

c ▶️02.19 Listen again and complete the chart with the words in the box.

> grammar   the classes   the teacher
> reading and writing   listening   the schedule

	Likes at the college	Needs to improve
Daniela		
Said		
Sakura		

d 💬🔊 Talk about the questions with other students.
1. What do you need to improve in English?
2. Why is this important for you?

e ▶️02.20 Listen to Kate talk about a competition at International College. What can you win?

f ▶️02.20 Listen again. Answer the questions.
1. Can students who don't go to International College enter the competition?
2. Is it OK to use a computer for the entry form?
3. Where can students get entry forms?

2 READING

a Look at the information about Daniela. Complete Part 1 of the form. Can you remember her nationality?

✉️ 📝 ☆ 🚩 ⊗

From: EIC Student Care
To: danielar@supermail.com

Dear Daniela,

We're looking forward to welcoming you to International College on July 6th.

You will be in class P1 and your teacher will be Kate Marks. We hope . . .

🌐 INTERNATIONAL COLLEGE COMPETITION ENTRY FORM

Part 1

First name: _____

Last name: *de las Torres*

Gender: ☐ female ☐ male

Nationality: _____

Cell phone (U.S.): (321) 555-0986

Email address: _____

Your class now: _____

Class start date: _____

Part 2

Why is English important for you?

> I work as a(n) ¹_____ in Mexico City. I love my job except for the ²_____! Every day they speak to me and ask me for information. I can't understand them, and it is difficult for me to answer. English is important to me because it helps me do my ³_____ well.

What do you want to improve in your English?

> I think my speaking in English is OK for my level. But ⁴_____ and understanding is still very difficult for me. I really want to stay an extra month at your school and improve my listening.

b Read Part 2 of Daniela's form. Complete it.

c ▶️02.21 Listen to Daniela again and check your answers.

3 WRITING SKILLS Spelling

a Read Daniela's first draft of her entry form. Cover page 26. Look at the example spelling problem. Find eight more spelling problems.

b Check (✓) when it's important to have correct spelling.

1 ☐ a first draft of a text
2 ☐ a final draft of a text
3 ☐ a text other people read
4 ☐ a text only you read

c Find and correct a spelling mistake in each sentence.

1 I really love swimming in the see.
2 Can you please right your name on the form?
3 I don't no the answer to this question.
4 Can you speak up? I can't here you.
5 Where can I bye bread?

d In what way are the incorrect and correct words in 3c the same?

4 WRITING

a Complete the form with your information.

b Use your ideas in 1d to write answers to the questions in Part 2.

c Switch forms with another student. Are your ideas in Part 2 the same?

INTERNATIONAL COLLEGE COMPETITION ENTRY FORM

Part 2

Why is English important for you?

> I work as a ~~trafic~~ traffic police offiser in Mexico City. I love my job except for the toorists! Every day they speak to me and ask me for informashion. I can't understand them, and it is dificult for me to anser. English is important for me becos it helps me do my job well.

What do you want to improve in your English?

> I think my speaking in English is OK for my level. I also find reading and writing pretty easy. But listning and understanding is still very hard for me. I really want to stay an extra month at your scool and improve my listening.

INTERNATIONAL COLLEGE COMPETITION ENTRY FORM

Part 1

First name:

Last name:

Gender: ☐ female ☐ male

Nationality:

Cell phone (U.S.):

Email address:

Your class now:

Class start date:

Part 2

Why is English important for you?

What do you want to improve in your English?

UNIT 2
Review and extension

1 GRAMMAR

a Complete the text with the correct form of the verb in parentheses.

I'm a college student, but I [1]_____ (work) in a clothing store every weekend. On Saturday I [2]_____ (start) work at 9:00 a.m., but on Sunday I [3]_____ (not start) until 11:00 a.m. My sister's a nurse, so she [4]_____ (not have) a normal schedule. She sometimes [5]_____ (work) all night, but she [6]_____ (not like) it. My parents are both teachers, so they [7]_____ (work) from Monday to Friday.

b Write possible questions for the answers.

1 **A** What _____? **B** I'm a receptionist.
2 **A** Do _____? **B** No, I don't. I work in a hospital.
3 **A** Do _____? **B** Yes, I do. It's great.
4 **A** When _____? **B** I start at 9 o'clock in the morning.
5 **A** Does _____? **B** Yes, he does. My husband is a teacher.
6 **A** Where _____? **B** He works in a high school.
7 **A** Does _____? **B** Yes, he does. He loves it.

c 💬📢 Practice the conversation in 1b with a partner. Answer about your life.

2 VOCABULARY

a Put the letters in parentheses in the correct order to complete the job.

1 n _____ e (s r u)
2 d _____ t (t e i s n)
3 p _____ t (l o i)
4 e _____ r (n n i e g e)
5 j _____ r (i o t a n)
6 p _____ r (o o h e h p r a t g)

b Write the times in words.

10:15 – (a) quarter after ten or ten fifteen
1 11:30   3 6:00   5 2:40
2 12:45   4 8:15   6 5:20

c Match 1–5 with a–e to complete the sentences.

1 Read the text and take
2 I'm not worried because I usually get good
3 I hope we have
4 He is worried because he often fails
5 I need to study for the final

a a break soon because I'm tired.
b important exams.
c notes on a piece of paper.
d exam next week.
e grades on tests.

3 WORDPOWER work

a Match sentences 1–3 with pictures a–c.

1 I **work in** a hospital.
2 I **work for** Larkin Computers
3 I **work as** a receptionist.

b Look at the phrases in **bold** in 3a. Match them with 1–3.

1 the job I do
2 the place of work
3 the company

c Is *work* a verb or a noun in sentences 1–5?

1 I start **work** at 8:00 a.m. each day.
2 She leaves **work** at about 6:00 p.m.
3 I can't talk to you now – I'm at **work**.
4 I'm an actor, but I'm out of **work** at the moment.
5 They go to **work** very early in the morning.

d Which *work* phrase in 3c do we use when … ?

a we don't have a job
b we are at the place we work

e Put the word in parentheses in the correct place in the sentence.

1 He works a nurse at night. (as)
2 We all work at 6:00 p.m. (start)
3 She'd like a job because now she's of work. (out)
4 She's a photographer and works *The Times*. (for)
5 When I'm work, I have no free time. (at)
6 We both work a large office downtown. (in)

f Write four sentences about people you know. Use *work* in different ways.

My brother works for a shoe store downtown.

⟳ REVIEW YOUR PROGRESS

How well did you do in this unit? Write 3, 2, or 1 for each objective.
3 = very well   2 = well   1 = not so well

I CAN ...	
talk about jobs	☐
talk about study habits	☐
ask for things and reply	☐
complete a form	☐

■ Talk about routines
■ Talk about technology in your life
■ Make plans
■ Write an informal invitation

UNIT 3

DAILY LIFE

GETTING STARTED

a 💬🔊 Look at the picture and answer the questions.

1 What country do you think this is? Why?
2 What time is it: morning or evening? Why?
3 Where do these people go when they get off the train?
4 What are their jobs?

b 💬🔊 In pairs, ask and answer the questions.

1 What things do you do every day?
  - take a bus or train
  - read your email
  - buy a cup of coffee
  - go for a walk

2 What do you do on a train or bus?
  - read
  - listen to music
  - talk to other passengers
  - use your phone

3A | SHE OFTEN TAKES AN ENGLISH CLASS

Learn to talk about routines
G Position of adverbs of frequency
V Time expressions; Common verbs

A Regular Office Job – Or Not?

Nora is 24, and she works in the marketing department of a large media company in Oslo. She works hard, but her company wants her to take breaks during the day, so she takes classes and sometimes plays with animals.

Nora gets up every weekday at 6:15 a.m. She eats breakfast, and then she leaves for work at 7:00 a.m. She usually arrives at work at about 8:15 a.m. – the trip takes more than an hour, and the trains are always crowded.

From 8:30 a.m. until 9:00 a.m., Nora reads her email and talks to coworkers. Then everyone in her department gets together for a short meeting. The boss tells everyone any important information, and workers can ask questions. Nora thinks it's a nice way to start the day – with everyone together.

At about 10:15 or 10:30, Nora usually takes a break. She often takes an English class, but she sometimes takes a knitting class. The company pays for these classes. At 12:30, she has lunch with her coworkers. Most people at the company bring lunch – called a "matpakke." It is usually a sandwich with fish or cheese.

In the afternoon, Nora always takes another break at about 3:00 p.m. She goes to the pet floor of her office building. The company has cats, dogs, and rabbits that workers play with on their breaks. Nora feeds the rabbits, and she often takes one of the dogs for a walk. The pet floor is Nora's favorite part of the office.

Nora never leaves the office before 5:30 p.m. She often has dinner with her coworkers at the company restaurant. The meal doesn't cost a lot of money. She goes home at 7:30 p.m.

1 READING

a 💬🔊 Look at the pictures of an office in Oslo and answer the questions. What do you think?

1 What kind of company is it?
2 What job do the people do?
3 Is their work life easy or hard?

b Read the article about Nora and answer the questions.

1 Is her work life easy or hard?
2 What is unusual about her work life?

c Read the article again. Are the sentences true or false? Correct the false ones.

1 Nora has her breakfast on the train to work.
2 Her trip to work takes a long time.
3 Early in the morning, Nora goes to a meeting with her coworkers.
4 During her morning break, she takes a knitting class and then an English class.
5 Nora likes the pet floor in her office building.
6 Nora always goes home at 5:30 p.m.

d 💬🔊 What are the good things about Nora's work life?

2 GRAMMAR Position of adverbs of frequency

a Look at this sentence from the article. The adverb of frequency is underlined.

She <u>usually</u> arrives at work at about 8.15 a.m.

<u>Underline</u> more adverbs of frequency in the article.

b Put the adverbs of frequency in the correct place on the time line.

~~sometimes~~   usually   never   often   always

```
                    sometimes
0% |————————|————————|————————|————————| 100%
```

c ≫ Now go to Grammar Focus 3A on p. 142.

d 💬🔊 Talk about the questions.

1 What do you always do in the morning?
2 What do you usually do in the afternoon?
3 What do you sometimes do in the evening?

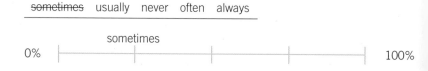

> I always get up at 6 o'clock.

> I often play tennis in the afternoon.

3 LISTENING

a 💬🎤 Ask and answer the questions.

1 Do you spend a lot of time with your family? Why / Why not?
2 What do you like doing with your family?

b ▶️ 03.02 Listen to Martin and Katherine. Answer the questions.

1 Do they talk about their jobs or free time?
2 What does Martin want the family to do?

c ▶️ 03.02 Listen again. Complete the schedule with the correct activity from the box.

Spanish class   band practice   work late   volleyball practice

d 💬🎤 Talk about the questions.

1 Is your family routine like the Lawson's, or is it different?
2 In your country, do families spend a lot of time together? What do they do?

The Lawson Family's Week

	Martin	Katherine	Liz	Pete
Monday				
Tuesday				
Wednesday				
Thursday				
Friday				

4 VOCABULARY Time expressions

a ▶️ 03.03 Complete the sentences. Listen and check.

twice   a   every   once

1 I go to my Spanish class _____ a week.
2 She goes to volleyball practice _____ a week, on Mondays and Thursdays.
3 He has band practice three times _____ week.
4 I work late _____ Tuesday.

b Underline the correct answer to complete the rule.

We put time expressions *before the verb* / *at the end of a sentence*.

c ▶️ 03.04 **Pronunciation** Listen to the question and answer. Notice the stressed words.

MARTIN   How <u>of</u>ten does she <u>go</u>?
KATHERINE   <u>Twice</u> a <u>week</u>, on <u>Mon</u>days and <u>Thurs</u>days.

d Which words do we usually stress? Choose the correct answer.

a Important words like time expressions and verbs.
b Less important words.

e ▶️ 03.05 Put the words in each sentence in the correct order to make a conversation. Listen and check.

A you and your family do / how often do / things together?
B a week / about once.
A you do / what do?
B we usually / to a restaurant / go on a picnic or.
A do that on / do you / weekends?
B but we sometimes / yes, every Sunday, / go to the movies.
A do anything else / do you?
B away for a weekend / a year we go / well, about twice.
A with your family / a nice time / it sounds like you have.

f ≫ Now go to Vocabulary Focus 3A on p. 165 for common verbs.

5 SPEAKING

a Think of a group of people you know well. Think of things you do together every day, week, or year. Take notes.

My parents – have a cup of tea every morning
Rob and Andy – usually go on vacation every June
My classmates – study English three times a week

b 💬🎤 Talk about what you do with the people you know well and how often. Look at the conversation in 4e to help you.

3B | IMAGINE YOU DON'T HAVE THE INTERNET

Learn to talk about technology in your life

G *do, go, have*
V Technology

1 READING

a How do you use the Internet? Check (✓) the things you sometimes do. Check (✓✓) the things you do every day.

- ☐☐ find information
- ☐☐ talk to friends
- ☐☐ send emails
- ☐☐ watch movies or TV
- ☐☐ post pictures
- ☐☐ play games
- ☐☐ buy things
- ☐☐ download music

b 💬 Talk about your answers with other students.

c Read the first part of the blog post.

1 Is it about … ?
   a using the Internet more
   b using the Internet less
2 What is unusual about the García family this month?

d Read the interview and answer the questions.

1 Which of the activities (a–f) does Chris do more without the Internet?
   a reading
   b going out
   c shopping
   d doing things with his father
   e chatting with friends
   f watching TV
2 What activities are now more difficult for Chris and his parents?

e 💬 Talk about the questions.

1 Would you like to live without the Internet? Why / Why not?
2 What do you think is good and bad about the Internet?

2 VOCABULARY Technology

a Match the words in the box with pictures 1–10.

> computer smartphone tablet smartwatch speaker
> keyboard printer headphones camera laptop

b ▶03.08 **Pronunciation** Listen and repeat the words in 2a. <u>Underline</u> the stressed syllable in each word.

c What are the people talking about? There is sometimes more than one answer.

1 I talk to my friends on it.
2 I use it to write emails.
3 I use these when I listen to music.
4 I often print out reports, so it's very useful.
5 I use it on the train.

TechBlog

HOME   REVIEWS   **FORUMS**   DOWNLOADS   LOGIN   SEARCH   💬 🔄 ☰ ✉

This month on TechBlog

These days, we all use the Internet – for everything. It's on our computers, our smartphones … it's everywhere. But what if you don't have the Internet? What if you can't send emails, you can't post photos, and you can't go online to get information?

How long could you live like that? A day? A week maybe, if you're on vacation? A month?

Here at Tech Blog we asked the García family in Richmond, Virginia, to live without the Internet for a whole month. Read our interview with Chris García, 17, about what it's like to go offline.

THE INTERVIEW

Chris, is your life different without the Internet?

Yes, it's really different! We usually get our TV through the Internet, so now I don't watch TV. And I usually go online to find information. But now we don't have the Internet, so I go to the library and do my homework there.

What about your parents?

It's not easy for them, either! My mom usually does her shopping online, but now she goes to the store every weekend. My dad likes to read the news online, but now he doesn't have the Internet, so he usually buys a newspaper. The good thing is, he doesn't do any work at home now, so he has more free time, and he plays chess with me.

What about friends?

That is a big problem. If I'm not on social media, I have no idea what my friends are doing. But I think life is good without the Internet. I can't chat online now, so now I go and see my friends, and we do things together. But a month without the Internet is enough. I can't wait to go back online again!

3 LISTENING

Don

Bella

Peter

a ▶ 03.09 Listen to Don's, Bella's, and Peter's conversations. Check (✓) the topics they talk about.

- ☐ groceries ☐ music ☐ TV ☐ sports
- ☐ movies ☐ clothes ☐ photos

b ▶ 03.09 Listen again. What gadgets do they talk about? How do they use them?

	Gadgets	How do they use them?
Don	1 2	
Bella	1	
Peter	1	

c ▶ 03.09 Listen again and check.

4 GRAMMAR do, go, have

a Choose the correct form of the verb in *italics*.

1 I *don't / doesn't* go to the movies very often.
2 My sister *do / does* all her grocery shopping online.
3 I *go / goes* and see my friends.
4 I *don't / not* do much shopping online.
5 She never *go / goes* to the grocery store.
6 He *don't / doesn't* do any work at home.

The García family

INTERNET FACT FILE

- The average teenager spends about nine hours a day online.
- Every minute, more than 500 hours of video are uploaded to YouTube.

b Complete the chart with the affirmative forms of the verbs.

	I / We / You / They	He / She / It
do	We _____ things together.	She _____ all her grocery shopping online.
go	I _____ to the library.	She _____ to the store every weekend.
have	I _____ my headphones right here.	Now he _____ more free time.

c Answer the questions.

1 Most verbs add *-s* after *he/she/it*. How are the verbs *do* and *go* different?
2 How is the verb *have* different?

d ≫ Now go to Grammar Focus 3B on p. 142.

e ▶ 03.11 **Pronunciation** Look at the verbs a–f. What sound do they have: 1, 2, or 3? Listen and check.

1 /ʌ/ like "b**u**t" 2 /oʊ/ like "n**o**" 3 /u/ like "t**oo**"
a do d goes
b does e doesn't
c go f don't

f Practice saying the sentences in 4b.

g ▶ 03.12 Look at the phrases in the box. Which follow *have*, which follow *go*, and which follow *do*? Then listen and check.

a laptop a camera yoga ~~online~~ to college
an e-book to the movies homework a car shopping

go online

h Write <u>three</u> sentences that are true for you, using phrases in the box in 4g.

1 use *have* or *don't have*
2 use *go* or *don't go*
3 use *do* or *don't do*

I have a laptop in my backpack.

i Write three questions with *go*, *have*, and *do* and phrases in the box in 4g.

Do you have a laptop?

5 SPEAKING

a Put the words in the correct order to make questions.

1 buy / you / do / what / ? 3 do / do you / when / it / ?
2 use it / how often / you / do / ? 4 where / you / go / do / ?

b Work with a partner. Ask and answer your questions in 4i. Then ask some of the questions from 5a to find out more.

> How often do you use it?

> Do you have a laptop?

> Every day, for my homework.

> Yes, I do.

3C EVERYDAY ENGLISH
How about next Wednesday?

Learn to make plans
S Thinking about what you want to say
P Main stress

1 LISTENING

a 💬🎙 Ask and answer the questions.

1 How often do you watch TV?
2 Are there shows you watch every week?
3 Do you have a favorite TV show? Who do you watch it with?

b ▶03.13 Listen to Part 1. Do Jessica and Priya like the same TV show?

c ▶03.13 Listen to Part 1 again. Are the sentences true or false?

1 The show Jessica wants to watch is *Best Cook*.
2 Priya doesn't watch this show very often.
3 Priya loves everything that has to do with food.

d ▶03.14 Listen to Part 2. What do they plan to do?

e ▶03.14 Answer the questions. Listen to Part 2 again and check your answers.

1 Why don't Priya and Jessica eat dinner at Jessica's apartment?
2 What does Jessica think about Priya's idea?
3 Which day does Jessica work late?
4 Which day do they decide to go out?

2 USEFUL LANGUAGE Making plans

a Match beginnings 1–6 with endings a–f.

1	Why	a	be great.
2	How	b	free next Friday?
3	Are you	c	don't we try it?
4	That'd	d	love to.
5	That works	e	about next Wednesday?
6	I'd	f	for me.

b Which questions in 2a do we use to make suggestions? Which sentences do we use to say *yes* to suggestions?

c Jessica says *no* to an idea. Underline the phrase that means *no*.

JESSICA I'm sorry, I can't. I need to work late next Wednesday.

d ▶03.15 Put the conversation in the correct order. Listen and check.

B ☐ I'm sorry, I can't. I'm busy this weekend.
A ☐1 Why don't we go to the movies?
B ☐ Yes, Monday's fine. That works for me.
A ☐ How about this Saturday?
A ☐ Are you free on Monday?
B ☐ The movies? I'd love to.

e 💬🎙 Practice the conversation in 2d. Then have similar conversations using your own ideas.

> Why don't we go for a picnic?

3 PRONUNCIATION Main stress

a ▶03.16 Listen to the sentences. Notice the main stress in each sentence.

1 That'd be <u>great</u>.   2 That's a <u>good</u> idea.   3 I'd <u>love</u> to.

b Choose the correct answer.

The words in 3a that have the main stress are ... .
a short and loud   b long   c long and loud

c ▶03.17 Listen to the sentences. Underline the main stress.

1 We'd love to.
2 That'd be good.
3 That's a great idea.
4 That'd be fantastic.

d 💬🎙 Practice the sentences in 3c.

4 CONVERSATION SKILLS
Thinking about what you want to say

a Look at the <u>underlined</u> phrases in the conversation. Choose the correct answer below.

PRIYA	How about next Wednesday?
JESSICA	<u>Hmm, maybe</u>. <u>Let me see</u>. I'm sorry, I can't. I need to work late next Wednesday.
PRIYA	Are you free next Friday?
JESSICA	<u>Hmm, possibly</u>. Friday's fine. 7:30?
PRIYA	That works for me!

Jessica uses the <u>underlined</u> phrases because they:
a have an important meaning in the conversation.
b give her time to think.

b **Pronunciation** Listen and notice how *Hmm* is pronounced. Do you have short words or sounds like this in your language?

c In pairs, ask and answer the questions. Think about your answer before you reply.

1 Are you free this weekend?
2 Do you want to get coffee after class?
3 Would you like to go to the movies tomorrow?
4 Why don't we do our homework together?

5 SPEAKING

a ≫ **Communication 3C** Student A look at the information below. Student B go to p. 132.

Conversation 1. Read your first card. Think about what you want to say. Then start the conversation with Student B.

> **1** You want to have a picnic on Saturday morning with Student B. Decide on the following and invite Student B.
> * where to have the picnic
> * what time
> * what you'd like to do/eat

b **Conversation 2.** Now look at your second card. Listen to Student B and reply.

> **2** You aren't free next Friday after work/school because you have an exercise class at the gym. You'd like to go out on Saturday night.

c Tell other students about the plans in each role play.

UNIT PROGRESS TEST

→ **CHECK YOUR PROGRESS**

You can now do the Unit Progress Test.

3D | SKILLS FOR WRITING
Can you join us?

Learn to write an informal invitation

W Inviting and replying

1 SPEAKING AND LISTENING

a 💬🗩 Ask and answer the questions.

1 Do you have family or friends in other countries or in other places in your country?
2 Where are they?
3 What do they do?
4 How often do you see them?

b ▶**03.19** Felipe from Ecuador talks about his family. Listen and number the places where he has family in the order you hear them.

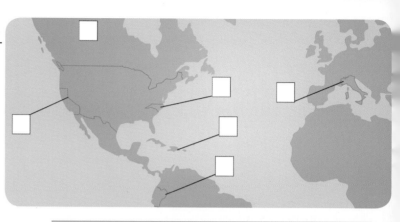

c ▶**03.19** Listen again. Correct the mistakes in the text below.

Felipe comes from a large family, and [1]they all live in Cuenca, Ecuador. [2]He doesn't have any brothers or sisters. His family keep in contact by Skype, and every [3]ten years they all meet in [4]Los Angeles. They stay [5]in a large hotel, and they have a big [6]meal. This [7]is only for people in the family – they [8]don't invite friends.

1 *They live in many different places.*

2 READING

a Read Felipe's emails to his friends. Why does he email them?

b Complete the information about the family party.
- Place
- How many days?
- Date
- Where to stay?

✉ 📝 ☆ ⚑   ⊗

Family party

From: FelipeB215@cup.org
To: CGarcia12@supermail.com

Hi Carlos,

[1]How are you? Hope the family's well.

[2]In September it's our family party again, and we all plan to meet in Cuenca as usual. [3]The party is from Friday, September 14th to Sunday the 16th. [4]Would you like to come? I hope so, as I'd love to see you. [5]Sergio (you know, my friend from school) says he has a spare bedroom, so you can stay at his house. [6]Please let me know if you would like to join us. I hope you can come!

Felipe

✉ 📝 ☆ ⚑   ⊗

Family party

From: FelipeB215@cup.org
To: Elena99@email.com

Hi Elena,

[1]How are things? Hope you like your new job.

[2]In September it's our family party again, and we all plan to meet in Cuenca as usual. [3]The party is from Friday, September 14th to Sunday the 16th. [4]Can you join us? I hope you can, as it would be great to see you. [5]Carolina (you know, my friend from school) says she has a spare bedroom, so you can stay at her house. [6]Please let me know if you can come. Hope you can make it!

Felipe

3 WRITING SKILLS Inviting and replying

a Read Felipe's email to Elena again. In which of sentences 1–6 does he … ?

a ☒4 invite Elena
b ☐ ask how she is
c ☐ ask her to reply
d ☐ give the reason for his message
e ☐ talk about where to stay
f ☐ give details of dates

b Compare sentences 1–6 in Felipe's emails to Carlos and Elena on p. 36. Underline phrases that are different.

c Check (✓) the correct questions to invite people.

1 ☐ Can you come?
2 ☐ Can you join?
3 ☐ Can you join us?
4 ☐ Can you to join us?
5 ☐ Would you like come?
6 ☐ Would you like to come?
7 ☐ Would you like to join us?

d Put the words in the correct order. Add question marks (?) and periods (.).

1 things / are / how
2 you / see / to / be / it / would / great
3 hope / it / can / you / make
4 to / I'd / you / love / see
5 are / you / how
6 I / can / come / you / hope

e Which sentences and questions in 3d mean the same?

f Read the emails from Carlos and Elena. Can they come?

✉ ✎ ☆ ⚑   ⊗

Re: Family party

From: CGarcia12@supermail.com
To: FelipeB215@cup.org

Hi Felipe,

It's good to hear from you, and thanks so much for the invitation. Yes, I'd love to come. I'm really looking forward to it. Please tell Sergio I'd love to stay with him if he has a spare room. See you soon.

Carlos

✉ ✎ ☆ ⚑   ⊗

Re: Family party

From: Elena99@email.com
To: FelipeB215@cup.org

Hi Felipe,

Great to hear from you, and thanks for the invitation. I'd love to come, but I'm afraid I can't. I have a business trip to New York that weekend, and I can't change it.

Hope you all have a great time, and hope to see you soon.

Keep in touch!

Elena

---

g Underline phrases in the emails from Carlos and Elena that mean:

1 I want to come.
2 I can't come.
3 Have a good time.

4 WRITING AND SPEAKING

a Plan a party or other event. Take notes.

- Where?   - When?   - Why?   - Who?

b 💬 Talk about your plan with other students.

> My party is at the Grand Hotel.

> It's for my brother's birthday.

> It's at 7 p.m. on Saturday.

c Write an invitation to your event to another student in your class. Use the emails on page 36 to help you.

d Switch invitations with another student and check the information.
Does it include the information in 4a?

e Write a reply to the invitation. Use the emails in 3f to help you. Give your reply back to the student who invited you.

UNIT 3
Review and extension

1 GRAMMAR

a Put the frequency adverbs in the correct place in the sentences.

1 He gets up at about 10 or 11. (often)
2 He goes to bed before 2:00 a.m. (never)
3 He studies all night. (sometimes)
4 He has black coffee and toast for breakfast. (usually)
5 He is away for a week or more. (often)
6 His windows are closed, even in summer. (always)

b Complete the text with the correct form of *have*, *go*, or *do*. Add *don't* or *doesn't* if necessary.

My brother and sister are very different. My brother and his wife ¹ _have_ office jobs, and they ² _____ a large house in Washington, D.C. Their house ³ _____ a big yard with a swimming pool. My brother ⁴ _____ to work at 7:00 every morning and comes home at 6:00 p.m., but then he often ⁵ _____ more work at home in the evening. They ⁶ _____ a lot of money, but they ⁷ _____ any free time. They ⁸ _____ much on the weekend because they are usually very tired, and they never ⁹ _____ on vacation.

My sister is a school teacher. She ¹⁰ _____ much money, but she ¹¹ _____ a lot of things in her free time. She ¹² _____ to a gym and plays basketball, she ¹³ _____ yoga, and she also ¹⁴ _____ to the movies and sees friends. She also ¹⁵ _____ a lot of free time in the summer. Every summer she ¹⁶ _____ to a different country, and she ¹⁷ _____ friends all over the world.

2 VOCABULARY

a Change the words in italics into a time expression.

1 She calls ~~on Tuesdays and Sundays~~. twice a week
2 There are English classes *in March, May, and October.*
3 We go on vacation *in June and in January.*
4 There's a boat *on Mondays, Wednesdays, and Saturdays.*
5 I check my email *before I start work and in the evening.*
6 Her mother calls on *Mondays, Tuesdays, Wednesdays, and Thursdays.*

b Write the names of the objects.

❶   ❷   ❸   ❹   ❺

❻   ❼   ❽   ❾   ❿

3 WORDPOWER Prepositions of time

a Match sentences 1–5 with pictures a–e.

1 He relaxes outside in the summer.
2 He works all the time – in the morning, in the evening, sometimes even at night.
3 He gets up at 6 a.m., but he finishes work at 1 p.m.
4 He works on weekday mornings, but on Sundays he gets up late.
5 In January he goes to a ski resort.

b Answer the questions.

1 Do we use *at*, *in*, or *on* with the following?
   a times
   b days
   c months
   d parts of days (morning, afternoon)
   e seasons (summer, winter)

2 How many examples of a–e can you find in 3a?

c Add *at*, *in*, or *on* in the correct place in these sentences. Some sentences may need more than one word.

1 I always get up 6:30 the morning weekdays.
2 It's usually cold here the winter, and it often snows January.
3 Are you free the weekend? I have tickets for a concert Saturday. It starts 7:30 p.m.

d When do you usually do these things? Write sentences.

1 get up   6 drink coffee or tea
2 go to bed   7 clean your apartment
3 have lunch   or house
4 go on vacation   8 cook meals
5 go shopping

e 💬 Ask and answer questions about when you usually do the things in 3d.

CAN DO OBJECTIVES

- Talk about the food you want
- Talk about the food you eat every day
- Arrive at and order a meal in a restaurant
- Write a blog post about something you know how to do

UNIT 4

FOOD

GETTING STARTED

a Look at the picture and answer the questions.

1 Do you think these people are friends or family?
2 What meal is this – breakfast, lunch, or dinner?
3 Is it the beginning, middle, or end of the meal?

b In pairs, ask and answer the questions.

1 How often do you eat together as a family?
2 What do you usually have for … ?
   - breakfast   - lunch   - dinner
3 What things do you talk about when you eat together?

4A | TRY SOME INTERESTING FOOD

1 READING

a 💬 Look at the pictures of places to buy food. Which one would you like to visit? Why?

b Read the article and match 1–3 with pictures a–c.

c Read the sentences. Where is each person?

JOSHUA	I love these pickled vegetables – they're great!
MADISON	I really only need a snack, but look at all the food I can buy!
SARAH	Now I know a new way to cook these potatoes.

d 💬 Talk about the questions.

1 Are there any markets in your town? What do they sell?
2 Where do you prefer shopping for food: in a market or a supermarket? Why?

2 GRAMMAR
Count and noncount nouns

a Look at the four nouns from the article. Which two have plural endings?

fruit   vegetables   tomatoes   cheese

b Complete the rule.

> We can't count some nouns (they are noncount nouns). We *always* / *never* add -s or -es.

c Look at the chart. Add food nouns from the article.

Count nouns (You can say *1, 2, 3 vegetables.*)	Noncount nouns (You can't say *1, 2, 3 fruits.*)
vegetables, tomatoes	fruit, cheese

WORLD MARKETS

Markets can be the best places to see the daily life of a city and to eat some fantastic local food. Today, read about different markets around the world.

COOK AS YOU SHOP

1 IF YOU WANT TO BUY FOOD AND LEARN HOW TO COOK IT at the same time, go to the Union Square Greenmarket in New York. It's open four days a week, and it has about 250,000 customers. Farmers from all over New York State sell food there. You can find different kinds of fruit and vegetables, such as potatoes, carrots, mushrooms, and tomatoes. The farmers show the best ways to cook the food, and you can even try the dishes they make for free!

A TASTE OF SÃO PAULO

2 THE MUNICIPAL MARKET OF SÃO PAULO, BRAZIL, is so large that people call it Mercadão (or big market). You can find almost any kind of food here, including fruit and vegetables, pasta, fresh meat, excellent cheese, spices, bread, chocolate, and more. Both tourists and locals like to shop and eat in this beautiful and historic building. You can try some of São Paulo's most famous food items here, such as the local sandwiches or pastries. There's something for everyone in the Mercadão!

KYOTO'S KITCHEN

3 ONE OF THE BEST PLACES TO TRY JAPANESE FOOD is in Kyoto, Japan. There you can find Nishiki Market. It's famous for its traditional Japanese food. It is over 700 years old, and its nickname is "Kyoto's kitchen." Most of the foods at Nishiki Market are local foods, so they come from Kyoto. The best chefs in Kyoto buy their ingredients here because the food is amazing! At Nishiki Market, you can try local foods such as tofu, pickled vegetables, grilled fish, and sweets.

3 VOCABULARY Food

a Match the food words with pictures 1–10.

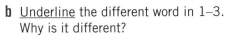

beans   lemons   chicken
mushrooms   onions   lamb
pears   steak   carrots   grapes

b Underline the different word in 1–3. Why is it different?

1 lemon   pear   carrot   grape
2 bean   lamb   onion   mushroom
3 steak   chicken   grape   lamb

c ▶04.01 **Pronunciation** Answer the questions. Then listen and check.

1 What is the same about the spelling of these words?
 • steak   • bean   • pear

2 Which word above has the same sound as these words?
 gr**ee**n /i/   h**ai**r /eə/   m**a**ke /eɪ/

d ▶04.02 What sound do the letters in **bold** have in the words in the box? Add the words to the sound groups below. Listen and check.

eat   wh**ere**   th**e**se   **ei**ght   r**ai**n   gr**ee**n   w**ea**r   d**ay**   f**ai**r

Sound 1 /eɪ/	Sound 2 /i/	Sound 3 /eə/
steak	bean	pear

e 💬🔊 Talk about the food you like and don't like.

f ≫ Now go to Vocabulary Focus 4A on p. 166 for more food vocabulary.

4 LISTENING

a 💬🔊 Ask and answer the questions.

1 Do you like cooking?
2 How often do you (or does someone in your family) buy food to cook?

b ▶04.06 Listen to Tom and Milly's conversation and answer the questions.

1 Does Milly want to cook?
2 Who doesn't want to go to the supermarket this weekend – Tom or Milly?
3 Where do they decide to buy food – at the supermarket or farmers' market?
4 Who says they can pay – Tom or Milly?

c ▶04.06 Listen again. Check (✓) the food on the shopping list that Tom and Milly need.

Meat:
☐ chicken   ☐ steak   ☐ fish

Vegetables:
☐ carrots   ☐ an onion   ☐ potatoes
☐ tomatoes   ☐ mushrooms

5 GRAMMAR *a / an, some, any*

a ▶04.07 Complete the sentences with the words in the box. Listen and check.

some   a/an   any (x2)

1 We have _____ potatoes.
2 Do we have _____ mushrooms?
3 And I need _____ onion.
4 I don't have _____ money.

b Complete the chart with *a*, *an*, *some*, and *any*.

	Count		Noncount
+	__a__ potato		_____ fruit
	_____ potatoes		
– / ?	_____ onion		_____ cheese
	_____ onions		

c ≫ Now go to Grammar Focus 4A on p. 144.

d ▶04.09 Complete the conversation with *a/an*, *some* or *any*. Listen and check.

SARAH Hello, I'd like [1]_____ lemon and [2]_____ onion, please.

VENDOR Just one?

SARAH Yes, and I'd like [3]_____ potatoes, too.

VENDOR Is this bag OK?

SARAH Yes, fine. Do you have [4]_____ small tomatoes?

VENDOR I'm sorry but I don't have [5]_____ small tomatoes.

SARAH OK, the big ones there are fine. Also I'd like [6]_____ cheese.

VENDOR I'm sorry, I don't sell cheese. Try that guy over there.

6 SPEAKING

a ≫ **Communication 4A** Student A go to p. 130. Student B go to p. 133.

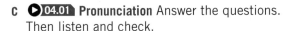

4B | HOW MUCH CHOCOLATE DO YOU NEED?

1 READING

a Answer the questions with other students.

1 Do you have any famous TV shows about cooking in your country?
2 Do you like the food they make on those shows? Why / Why not?
3 Do you know the chef in the picture?
4 Read the information about Aarón Sánchez. Would you like to try his food? Why / Why not?

b Read Josh's email to his father. Answer the questions.

1 Who lives in New Orleans – Josh or his dad?
2 Which restaurant does Josh want to go to?
3 Why does Josh want to go to this restaurant?

c Read his dad's reply. Does he want to go to *Johnny Sánchez*?

d Read his dad's email again. What does he think about these things? <u>Underline</u> the correct answers.

1 Aarón Sanchéz's food: *boring / different*
2 His wife's food: *normal / strange*
3 The restaurant: *expensive for him / expensive for Josh*

e Talk about the questions.

1 Do you like going to restaurants with your family? Or do you prefer to eat at home? Why / Why not?
2 Do you like trying new food? Why / Why not?

Introducing... Aarón Sánchez

Who is Aarón Sánchez?

A famous chef and TV star, Sánchez has written two cookbooks and owns a Mexican restaurant called *Johnny Sánchez* in New Orleans.

What's he famous for?

Aaron makes creative dishes, such as lamb enchiladas and a skirt steak taco with grilled avocado. You can try making his crab tostadas – the recipe is in his cookbook *Simple Food Big Flavor*!

---

visit

From: Josh1994@supermail.com
To: MrBLJohnson@supermail.com

Hi Dad,

When you come to New Orleans next week, I want to take you out to dinner. Would you like to go to Aarón Sanchéz's restaurant *Johnny Sánchez*? It looks fun and I can pay! Do you remember my friend Pete? Well, he goes to *Johnny Sánchez* every time his parents are in town. He always has the oyster tacos, and he says they're amazing! And his mom says the grilled fish is great, too. I really want to take you there!

Josh

Re: visit

From: MrBLJohnson@supermail.com
To: Josh1994@supermail.com

Hi Josh,

Thanks for the invitation to *Johnny Sánchez*. I know about that guy Aarón Sánchez from TV. His food is interesting, and it's certainly kind of unusual. But really I'm happy to go to a normal restaurant and have some roasted chicken and boiled potatoes, like your mom makes at home. Or I'm also fine with a can of soup at your place. It's a nice idea to go to the restaurant, but it will be expensive for you. You don't need to do anything special for me.

Dad

2 VOCABULARY Cooking

a Read the cooking instructions 1–5 and match them with the pictures a–e.

1 **Fry** the onions in a little oil.
2 Put water and rice in a pot and **boil** for 12 minutes.
3 **Grill** the chicken for 10 minutes until it's brown.
4 Put some herbs on the chicken and **roast** it in the oven.
5 **Bake** the bread in a hot oven for 30 minutes.

b ▶04.10 Complete the chart. Use verbs from 2a and adjectives from Josh's dad's email. Listen and check.

Verb	Adjective
boil	
	fried
	grilled
	baked
roast	

c Complete the examples with adjectives in 2b.
- add -ed   *boiled*
- add -d   _____
- changes -y to -ied   _____

d 💬 Talk about the questions.
1 Which kinds of cooking do you think are healthy? Which do you think are unhealthy?
2 Choose two kinds of food. What is your favorite way to cook that food?

e ≫ Now go to Vocabulary Focus 4B on p. 166 for containers vocabulary.

3 LISTENING

a ▶04.12 Listen to Olivia and Harry talk about recipes. Check (✓) which two recipes they choose.

☐ Superb mashed potatoes   ☐ Seared tuna tostada
☐ Black bean soup   ☐ Chocolate coffee sauce

b ▶04.12 Listen again. Underline the correct food words in the instructions for Olivia and Harry.
1 Olivia needs *potatoes / chips* and *cream / butter*.
2 She needs to *boil / roast* the ingredients.
3 Harry needs *honey / sugar*, *coffee beans / black coffee*, and *milk chocolate / dark chocolate*.
4 He needs to *grill / boil* the ingredients.

c 💬 Which recipe would you like to make?

4 GRAMMAR Quantifiers: *much, many, a lot (of)*

a ▶04.13 Complete the sentences with the correct words in the box. Listen and check.

much   a lot   many   a little

1 That's _____ _____ of butter.
2 How _____ chocolate? Only _____
_____ – 50 grams.
3 How _____ grams of butter?

b Look at the phrases in italics in 1–3. Can you use them with count *(C)* or noncount *(N)* nouns, or both *(B)*?
1 **A** *How much* butter does Olivia need?
   B *A lot / Quite a bit / A little / Not much.*
2 **A** *How many* beans does Harry need?
   B *A lot / Quite a few / A few / Not many.*
3 I need *a lot of* potatoes and chocolate.

c ≫ Now go to Grammar Focus 4B on p. 144.

d ▶04.16 Complete the conversation. Then put the conversation in order. Listen and check.
B ☐ A ¹_____ – about five or six pieces.
A ☐ Really? That's not ²_____ water.
B ☐ About two.
A ☐ And what about drinks? How
     ³_____ glasses of water do you have a day?
A ☐1 How ⁴_____ fruit do you eat a day?

e 💬 Do you think that Speaker B in 4d is healthy or unhealthy? Why?

5 SPEAKING

a Write questions to ask your partner about the food they eat.

Do you eat much fish?
What fruit do you like?
How many slices of bread do you eat a day?
How much rice do you eat a week?

b 💬 Ask your questions and write down your partner's answers.

c 💬 Go to page 131 and read about food that is healthy to eat every day. Look at your partner's answers and decide if your partner eats in a healthy way.

4C EVERYDAY ENGLISH
Do we need a reservation?

1 LISTENING

a 💬 Ask and answer the questions.

1 How often do you go to a restaurant?
2 What kind of restaurants do you like?
3 Do people eat out a lot in your country?

b 💬 Work in pairs. Look at picture a. Why do you think the restaurant is empty? Choose an answer.

1 The restaurant isn't open.
2 People think the server isn't very nice.
3 It's very early.

c ▶ 04.17 Listen to Part 1 and check your answers in 1b.

d ▶ 04.17 Listen to Part 1 again. Are the sentences true or false? Correct the false sentences.

1 They have a reservation for two people.
2 They want a table by the door.
3 Emily finds it difficult to choose a table.

---

2 USEFUL LANGUAGE
Arriving at a restaurant

a Read the sentences. Who is the server – A or B?

A No problem.
B Can we have a table by the window?
A Good evening. Do you have a reservation?
A Yes, of course. This way, please.
B No, we don't. We'd like a table for four.

b ▶ 04.18 Put the sentences in 2a in the correct order. Listen and check your answers.

c 💬 Practice the conversation with a partner.

d 💬 Change what B says in 2a. Use the sentences below.

1 We'd like a table outside.
2 Yes, we have a reservation for two people. The name's Morton. But we're twenty minutes late.

3 LISTENING

a Read the restaurant menu. Which dish(es) would you like? Why?

> I'd like the salad and the spaghetti because I don't like meat.

> I'd like the Thai chicken curry because I really like Asian food.

b ▶ 04.19 Listen to Part 2.

1 What do Tim and Emily order?
2 Who can't decide what they want to have?

c 💬 Do you sometimes find it difficult to choose at a restaurant? Why / Why not?

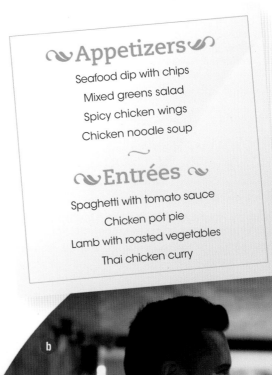

❧ Appetizers ❧

Seafood dip with chips
Mixed greens salad
Spicy chicken wings
Chicken noodle soup

~

❧ Entrées ❧

Spaghetti with tomato sauce
Chicken pot pie
Lamb with roasted vegetables
Thai chicken curry

4 USEFUL LANGUAGE
Ordering a meal in a restaurant

a Complete the conversations from Part 2 with the words in the box.

> have   then   with   I'd   like

SERVER	What would you like for your appetizer?
EMILY	I'll ¹_____ chicken wings, please.
SERVER	And for your entrée?
EMILY	²_____ like the spaghetti.
SERVER	And for your appetizer, sir?
TIM	I'd ³_____ the chicken noodle soup, please.
SERVER	Chicken noodle soup to start.
TIM	And ⁴_____ for my entrée I'll have the lamb.
SERVER	Would you like rice ⁵_____ that?
TIM	Yes, please.

b Check (✓) the two phrases we use when we want to order food in a restaurant.

1 ☐ I have   3 ☐ I'd want
2 ☐ I'd like   4 ☐ I'll have

c ▶04.20 Put the words in the correct order to make sentences. Listen and check.

1 salad / my / I'd / appetizer / for / like
2 entrée / I'll / my / spaghetti / for / have
3 I'd / rice / chicken / like / with / curry

5 PRONUNCIATION Word groups

a ▶04.21 Listen to the sentences. In each sentence there are two or more word groups. Write ‖ where you hear the beginning of a new word group.

1 For my <u>appetizer</u>, ‖ I'd like raw <u>fish</u>.
2 And I'll have steak <u>tacos</u> for my <u>entrée</u>.
3 I'd like cucumber <u>salad</u> for my <u>appetizer</u>.

b ▶04.21 Listen again. Notice the main stress in each word group.

c ▶04.22 Write ‖ where you hear the start of a new word group. Listen and check.

For my <u>appetizer</u>, ‖ I'll have <u>tomato</u> soup. And then I'd like a <u>cheeseburger</u> for my <u>entrée</u>. And I'll have some <u>fries</u> with my <u>burger</u>.

d 💬 In pairs, practice saying the order in 5c.

6 CONVERSATION SKILLS
Changing what you say

a Look at the two sentences from the conversation. <u>Underline</u> the phrases Emily uses when she wants to change what she wants to say.

1 **EMILY**   What about the one on the right?
  TIM   OK, if you like that one …
  EMILY   Maybe not. The one on the left is fine …

2 **EMILY**   I'll have the chicken wings to start. No, wait. I'll have chicken salad.

b ▶04.23 Complete the sentences. Listen and check.

1 I'll have seafood dip. Maybe _____.
  I'd like the chicken wings.
2 I'd like spaghetti, I think. No, _____. I'll have the chicken pot pie.

7 SPEAKING

a 💬 Work in groups of three or four. Use the menu on page 44. Write one more appetizer and one more entrée.

b 💬 You are at a restaurant. Take turns being the server and the customer. Order a meal from the menu. Use phrases from 4a to help you. Practice changing what you say when you order.

✓ **UNIT PROGRESS TEST**

➡ **CHECK YOUR PROGRESS**

You can now do the Unit Progress Test.

4D | SKILLS FOR WRITING
Next, decide on your menu

1 SPEAKING AND LISTENING

a 💬🔊 Ask and answer the questions.

1 Which of the dishes in pictures a–d would you like to eat?
2 Can you make any dishes like these?
3 Who does most of the cooking in your house: you or another person? Why?

b ▶️04.24 Four people talk about cooking. Listen and <u>underline</u> the correct answers.

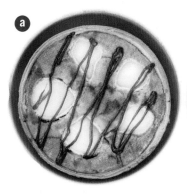

Name	Talks about		
Jake	*himself / his wife*	a *good / bad* cook	picture *a / b / c / d*
Rosa	*herself / her husband*	a *good / bad* cook	picture *a / b / c / d*
Johanna	*herself / her father*	a *good / bad* cook	picture *a / b / c / d*
Marco	*himself / his mother*	a *good / bad* cook	picture *a / b / c / d*

c ▶️04.24 Listen again. Answer the questions.

1 Who always wants to eat more?
2 Who can only make one thing?
3 Who doesn't understand how you can make a really good dish from only a few things?
4 Who enjoys their own food?

d Think of someone you know who is a good cook. Take notes.

• Who?   • Why?   • What dishes?

e 💬🔊 Ask and answer about the good cook you know.

> Who do you know who is a good cook?

> My father – he's a great cook.

> Why is your father a good cook?

> He can cook many different things.

> What does he make?

> He makes fantastic chicken salad.

2 READING

a Read the blog description. Who is it for?

a people who know how to cook very well
b people who want to learn how to cook

JAKE COOKS!

Hi, everyone, and welcome to my cooking blog.

I'm not a good cook, but I want to improve. I just want to learn how to cook simple dishes and eat well. I don't want to cook difficult things, and I don't want to be a famous chef. In this blog, I want to tell you about the help I get from my family and friends and the things I try out. So if you want to be a better cook, but not a chef, then maybe I can help you!

b Read the blog post below. What does Jake talk about?

a the food he eats

b planning a dinner

c Read the blog post again. Are the sentences true or false? Correct the false sentences.

1 Jake hopes the blog can help other people plan dinner for friends.

2 It's not a good idea to invite a lot of people for dinner.

3 It's always fun to try a new dish because friends can tell you if it's good or not.

4 Choose the night of the dinner and then tell your friends.

5 It helps to do all the cooking before your friends come.

d 💬 Do you prefer making meals for other people or going to someone's home for a meal? Why?

3 WRITING SKILLS Making the order clear

a In Jake's blog post, the words *first* and *next* help make the order clear. Underline two more phrases in the blog post that also make the order clear.

b Answer the questions.

Which two phrases can we change with *then*?

What punctuation do we use after these phrases?

c Read the recipe for a bean salad. Only sentences 1 and 5 are in the correct order. Put the other sentences in the correct order.

1	Cook the beans in hot water with a little salt.
	Add salt and pepper and mix everything together.
	Put lemon and oil on the warm beans – not too much.
	Leave the beans until they are warm.
5	Place the bean salad in a nice bowl and serve to your guests.

d Add the words in the box to the sentences in 3c.

first   after that   next   then   finally

First, cook the beans in hot water ...

4 WRITING

a Plan a blog post about something you know how to do.

• What are good ideas to improve?

• What's a good order to do things?

b Write your blog post. Use *My food – shared!* to help you.

c Switch blog posts with another student and check to see if the order is clear.

JAKE COOKS!

My food – shared!

Added at 12:47 today

Do you like the idea of cooking dinner for friends? Here are my ideas for planning a dinner for friends – I hope you find them useful . . .

First, think about how many people you want to invite. Don't invite too many – I think four people is a good number.

Next, call or text to invite your friends and agree on a night that's good for everyone.

After that, decide on your menu. Only choose food that you know how to prepare. Don't choose new and difficult dishes – it's just too hard. Your friends know that you are not a chef and your house is not a restaurant!

Finally, on the day of the dinner, you need a lot of time to prepare everything – the food and the table. (The weekend is good because you have all day to prepare.) If everything is ready before your guests arrive, you can enjoy the dinner much more.

Cooking for friends can be easy and fun. I hope it is for you!

UNIT 4
Review and extension

1 GRAMMAR

a Correct the words (1–10) that are wrong.

There's a very good market near my home. I always go there to buy ¹*food*. Some stalls sell ²*vegetable* and ³*fruits*. I usually buy ⁴*potato* and ⁵*onions* there because they're very cheap. At my favorite stall, a woman sells ⁶*butters*, ⁷*cream*, and ⁸*egg* from her own farm. There is also a building where they sell ⁹*fishes* and ¹⁰*meat*.

b Underline the correct answers.

1 Do we have *an* / *any* onions?
2 How *much* / *many* coffee do you drink?
3 How *much* / *many* bananas would you like?
4 Can you buy *a* / *some* spaghetti?
5 Is there *any* / *many* milk in the fridge?
6 How *a lot of* / *much* money do you have?

c Choose the correct answer.

1 I don't have _____ money, but I can buy a cup of coffee.
  a some   b many   c much
2 There aren't _____ bananas. Let's buy some more.
  a much   b many   c some
3 The party's going to be great – _____ people want to come.
  a much   b a lot of   c any
4 He has _____ good books about food and cooking.
  a some   b much   c any

2 VOCABULARY

a Match the words in the box with 1–5. Then add one more word to each group.

| pear | chicken | grape | cheese | grilled |
| lamb | potato | boiled | carrot | yogurt |

1 kinds of meat
2 vegetables
3 kinds of fruit
4 things that come from milk
5 ways of cooking food

b Look at 1–9. Which are normal (✓) and which are unusual (or impossible) (✗)?

1 grilled steak ✓
2 roasted butter ✗
3 boiled egg
4 grilled rice
5 fried fish
6 fried grapes
7 roasted chicken
8 fried mushrooms
9 boiled potatoes

3 WORDPOWER *like*

a Read the three conversations. Which one matches the picture?

1 **A** What kind of fruit **do you like**?
  B I like most kinds of fruit, but not bananas.
2 **A** What vegetables **would you like**?
  B I'd like potatoes and carrots, please.
3 **A** We want to have a party. **Would you like** to join us?
  B Yes, thanks. I'd love to.

b Look at the questions in 3a. Which question … ?

1 is about what B wants now
2 invites B to go somewhere
3 is about what B likes in general (not just now)

c Match a–c with similar meaning 1–3 in 3b.

a I don't like *Amy's House*. I think it's a terrible show.
b Would you like to come to my birthday party?
c I'd like two lemons, please.

d Match the words in **bold** in 1–4 with meanings a–d.

1 **What's it like** to live without the Internet?
2 They don't have a computer. I couldn't live **like that**.
3 I eat a lot of fruit, **like** apples, pears, melons, and bananas.
4 She's 20 and she studies Russian, just **like** me.

a the same as   b for example
c how is it   d in that way

e Write a question or a sentence with *like* for each situation.

1 Invite a friend to the movies on Friday.
2 You're in a supermarket. Ask for some apples.
3 You're a server in a café. A customer says "A coffee, please."
4 Someone is a guest in your home. You want to know what to cook for him/her.
5 At a party, someone says he/she lives in New York. Ask him/her about the city.

f 💬 Ask and answer the questions in 3e with a partner.

🔄 REVIEW YOUR PROGRESS

How well did you do in this unit? Write 3, 2, or 1 for each objective.
3 = very well   2 = well   1 = not so well

I CAN …	
talk about the food I want	☐
talk about the food I eat every day	☐
arrive at and order a meal in a restaurant	☐
write a blog about something I know how to do	☐

PLACES

UNIT **5**

GETTING STARTED

a 💬🔊 Talk about the picture. Which ideas do you think are true?

1 A family lives here.
2 People go here for a quiet weekend.
3 Wild animals live inside.
4 You can stay here on vacation.
5 People use it when it rains a lot and the river is high.

b 💬🔊 In pairs, ask and answer the questions.

1 Why is this a good place for a home?
2 Why is it a bad place?
3 What is a "good home"?
  Here are some ideas:
  ● It's in a quiet place.   ● It has a lot of rooms.
  ● It's expensive.   ● It has a yard.
  ● It's downtown.   ● It's modern.

49

5A | THERE AREN'T ANY PARKS OR SQUARES

1 READING

a 💬 Look at the pictures of Whittier, Alaska. How do you think the town is unusual?

b Read the article and check your answer.

UNUSUAL TOWNS
Whittier, Alaska

Do you want to go to the grocery store? In most towns you walk down a street, or maybe you go by bus. Do you need to go to work? In most places, you probably take a bus or go by car. But in Whittier, you never go outside when you do these things. That's because almost the whole town is in one huge building with fourteen floors. In this one building, there are stores, there's a church, there's a police station, and there's even a hospital. There are also many apartments for the people who live there, and there are offices where people work, all under one roof. Only 220 people live in Whittier, so there isn't a college or university in the town, but there's one school for all the children. And of course everything is inside, so there aren't any parks or squares, and there aren't any street cafés like in other towns.

So why is it like that? Well, Whittier is on the coast of Alaska, and the weather is terrible most of the year. In summer it often rains, and there's a lot of snow in winter (about seven meters), and also very strong winds. So people in Whittier are happy to stay inside most of the time.

It isn't easy to get to and from Whittier because there isn't a normal road. The only way to get there on land is through a long tunnel. It's 3 km long, and it's very narrow, so cars can go through it once every hour. And the tunnel closes at 10:30 p.m. After that, you have to stay the night in Whittier and leave in the morning.

Do people like to live there? Yes, they do! As one man from Whittier says: "It's safe here, it's quiet, and people are friendly. And there are beautiful mountains and forests all around. I love it here!"

c Can you do these things in Whittier?

1 go to work by bus
2 sit outside in a café
3 buy groceries
4 go for a walk in July
5 go for a walk in January
6 drive to Whittier at 3:00 in the morning

d 💬 Talk about the questions.

1 Would you like to visit Whittier?
   Why / Why not?
2 Would you like to live there?

Mexico City

2 VOCABULARY Places in a city

a <u>Underline</u> twelve words in the article for places in a town or city. Which are ... ?

1 buildings or in buildings   2 outside

b ≫ Now go to Vocabulary Focus 5A on p. 164.

c 💬 Work with other students. Write words for more places in a city. Think of:

- places to go in the evening
- things to see
- places to relax in the daytime

d 💬 Talk about three places you like in your town or city.

3 GRAMMAR *there is / there are*

a Complete the sentences from the article with *there's*, *there are*, *there isn't*, or *there aren't*.

1 _____ any parks or squares.
2 _____ a church.
3 _____ much to do around Whittier.
4 _____ offices where people work.

b Complete the chart with forms of *there is* or *there are*.

+	–
There _'s_ a police station.	There ____ a normal road.
There ____ a few stores.	There ____ any street cafés.

c Match questions 1–4 about Whittier with answers a–d.

1 Is there a road to Whittier?
2 Is there a college?
3 Are there any parks in the town?
4 Are there mountains near the town?

a Yes, there are. They're very beautiful.
b Yes, there is. It goes through a tunnel.
c No, there isn't, but there's a school.
d No, there aren't. The town is inside a building.

d Complete the chart with forms of *there is* or *there are*.

Yes/No questions	Short answers	
____ ____ a good hotel in the town?	Yes, there ____.	No, there ____.
____ ____ any good restaurants?	Yes, ____ ____.	No, ____ ____.

e ≫ Go to Grammar Focus 5A on p. 146.

f ▶ 05.04 **Pronunciation** Listen and repeat.

buildings	trains	markets	cafés
parks	there's	restaurants	maps

Which words end with ... ?

1 the sound /s/   2 the sound /z/

g ≫ **Communication 5A** Student A go to p. 131. Student B go to p. 132.

4 SPEAKING

a ▶ 05.05 Tom asks his friend, Gabriela, about visiting Mexico City, her hometown. Complete the conversation with the correct form of *there is* or *there are*. Listen and check your answers.

TOM Is Mexico City a good place to visit?
GABRIELA Oh, it's a fantastic city to visit. [1]_____ a lot of interesting old buildings, and [2]_____ some beautiful squares.
TOM [3]_____ any good restaurants?
GABRIELA Yes, [4]_____, and the street food is good, too.
TOM What about coffee shops? [5]_____ any good coffee shops?
GABRIELA Oh yes, [6]_____ a lot of good coffee shops. The coffee's very good in Mexico.
TOM And what about the geography? [7]_____ a large river in Mexico City?
GABRIELA No, [8]_____ a river, but [9]_____ a lot of mountains nearby, including volcanoes.

b 💬 Work in groups of four: Pair A and Pair B.

stores and markets	things to see
buses and trains	restaurants and cafés
parks	famous buildings	bridges

Pair A: You are visitors to a town or city. Write questions to ask about the things in the box.

Is there a ...? Are there any ...?
Can I ...? Where can I ...?

Pair B: Think about a town or city that you know well. Take notes about the things in the box.

The city is great to visit because ... and ...
There's a famous ... It's called ...
There are a lot of ...

c 💬 Use the conversation in 4a and your notes in 4b to have a conversation.

Pair A: Ask about the town.
Pair B: Answer the questions about the town.

Learn to describe rooms and furniture in your home

G Possessive pronouns and possessive 's

V Furniture

1 VOCABULARY Furniture

a 💬 Ask and answer the questions.

1 Do you live in a house or an apartment?
2 How old is your home?
3 Where can you buy furniture in your country?

> My apartment is very old.

> I always buy furniture online.

b Read the advertisement for a furniture shop. Who is the store for?

a people who like expensive furniture
b people who don't want to spend too much money on furniture

c Match the words in the box with pictures a–l.

---
mirror   washing machine   bookcase   curtains
sink   nightstand   armchair   wardrobe   lamp
dresser   stove   couch

---

d ▶ 05.06 Pronunciation Listen to the pronunciation of the letters in bold. Which words have the same sounds?

1 fur**ni**ture
2 **wa**rdrobe
3 **cur**tains
4 d**oor**
5 y**our**
6 h**er**

e Match *floor*, *nurse*, *verb*, and *store* with words with the same sounds in 1d.

f Look at the room you are in now. Write a list of the furniture in it.

g 💬 Compare your list with a partner.

> What do you have?

> I have …

FURNITURE CITY

NEW APARTMENT?
Do you have all the furniture you need?

We sell new and second-hand furniture:
• beds • chairs • couches • wardrobes • bookcases • dresser

From classic to crazy – we have all the furniture you need.

It's all good quality at a low price.

FURNITURE C I T Y   Buy online or in store

2 LISTENING

a 💬🔊 Ask and answer the questions.

1 Which is your favorite room in your home?
2 Do you have a favorite piece of furniture?

b ▶️ 05.07 Jim's sister, Eva, comes to visit him in his new apartment. Listen to their conversation. Which rooms does Jim show Eva?

a the kitchen   c the bathroom
b the living room   d the bedroom

c ▶️ 05.07 Listen again and write down the furniture they talk about in each room.

room 1 _____
room 2 _____

d What does Eva think about the furniture in Jim's apartment?

3 GRAMMAR
Possessive pronouns and possessive *'s*

a ▶️ 05.08 Complete the conversation with words from the box. Listen and check your answers.

your   Mom and Dad   David's   mine
yours   of   David   Mom and Dad's

EVA I love that armchair.
JIM Yes, it's ... interesting.
EVA Is it ¹_____?
JIM No, it's ²_____. He's my roommate.
EVA I love it. That mirror over there. Is that ³_____?
JIM Well, yes, but really it's ⁴_____ now.

b Check (✓) the correct sentences.

1 ☐ It's the apartment of Jim.
2 ☐ It's Jims apartment.
3 ☐ It's Jim's apartment.
4 ☐ It's my parent's apartment.
5 ☐ It's the apartment of my parents.
6 ☐ It's my parents' apartment.

c Look at the sentences and answer the questions.

Whose mirror is that?   a *It's my mirror.*
                          b *It's mine.*

1 Do we need to repeat *mirror* in the answer?
2 Which answer is better?

d Complete the sentences with the words in the box.

yours   hers   mine   his   theirs

1 It's my bed.   → It's _____.
2 It's your lamp.   → It's _____.
3 It's her couch.   → It's _____.
4 It's their mirror. → It's _____.
5 It's his chair.   → It's _____.

e ≫ Now go to Grammar Focus 5B on p. 146.

f ▶️ 05.12 Read about Antonio's apartment. Complete the text with the words in the box. Listen and check your answers.

sister's   parents'   mine (x3)
mother's   hers   yours

I live in an apartment with seven rooms. It's not ¹_____ – it's my ²_____. In my bedroom, there's a really big bookcase that I love. It's my ³_____, but she doesn't live at home now, so I don't think it's ⁴_____ anymore – it's ⁵_____ now. My dad has a study with a beautiful old desk. It's really my ⁶_____, but Dad always says to Mom, "It's not ⁷_____ now, it's ⁸_____."

4 SPEAKING

a Write four sentences about your home, the furniture in it, and whose furniture it is. Look at Antonio's words in 3f to help you.

b 💬🔊 Read your sentences to a partner. Listen to your partner's sentences and try to remember the information.

c 💬🔊 Tell your partner what you remember about their home. Who can remember the most?

Jim's roommate, David

Jim and Eva

> In the living room there's a very large couch.

> No, there are two large couches.

> The lamp in your bedroom is your brother's.

> Yes, that's right.

5C EVERYDAY ENGLISH
Is there a theater near here?

Learn how to ask for and give directions
- **S** Checking what other people say
- **P** Sentence stress

1 LISTENING

a 💬🔊 Answer the questions about the pictures.

1 Where do you think Jess and Landon want to go? Say why.
   a a theater   c the gym
   b a meeting
2 There's a problem. What do you think it is?

b ▶️**05.13** Listen to Part 1 and check your answers in 1a.

2 CONVERSATION SKILLS
Checking what other people say

a ▶️**05.14** Look at the sentences from Part 1 and answer the questions.

JESS Are you **sure**?
LANDON I think so.

JESS Are you **positive** it's on South Street?
LANDON Yes.

1 Are the questions still correct if we switch the two words in **bold**?
2 Why does Jess ask the questions? Choose the correct answer.
   a She agrees with Landon.
   b She wants to check something with Landon.

3 LISTENING

a 💬🔊 When you're lost, what do you usually do? Choose one idea.

1 Look again for the correct street on your phone.
2 Continue down the street and look for the correct street.
3 Ask someone for help to find the correct street.

b ▶️**05.15** Listen to Part 2. Do Jess and Landon have the same idea as you in 3a?

c ▶️**05.15** Listen to Part 2 again. Are the sentences true or false? Correct the false sentences.

1 Jess and Landon want to find a theater that is on the corner of Park Road and South Street.
2 The man on the street says there's a theater 150 meters away.

d 💬🔊 Work in pairs. Look at picture c. Jess and Landon find a theater, but there's another problem. What do you think it is?

e ▶️**05.16** Listen to Part 3. Answer the questions.

1 Do they find the correct theater?
2 Does the woman they talk to know where South Street is?

c ▶️**05.13** Listen to Part 1 again. Choose the correct answer.

1 The street name on Jess's phone is … .
   a Bedford Street   b Park Road
2 Jess says South Street is … .
   a off Park Road   b off North Street
3 Landon doesn't want to be … .
   a too early   b late

f ▶05.16 Listen to Part 3 again. Follow the woman's directions. Write *South Street* on the map.

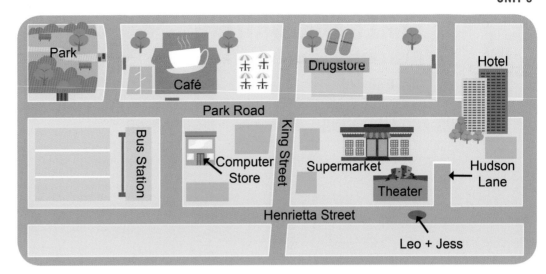

4 USEFUL LANGUAGE
Asking for and giving directions

a Complete the questions with the words in the box.

tell   where   there   how

1 Is _____ a bank near here?
2 Can you _____ us how to get to South Street?
3 _____ do I get to Park Road?
4 _____ can I find a supermarket?

b Look at the phrases for giving directions. Change the words in **bold** with the words in the box.

a supermarket   on   left

1 Go straight **down** this road.
2 The bank is on your **right**.
3 Go straight until you come to **Park Road**.

c Match the directions with maps a–b.

1 Turn right **at** the bus station.
2 Turn right **onto** Park Road.

d ▶05.17 Complete the conversation with the words in the box. Listen and check.

go (x3)   turn (x2)   get   can   come

A Excuse me, ¹_____ you tell me how to ²_____ to the park?
B Yes, ³_____ straight and ⁴_____ right at the corner.
A Is that right onto King Street?
B Yes and ⁵_____ down King Street until you ⁶_____ to Park Road. Then ⁷_____ left.
A Left onto Park Road?
B Yes and ⁸_____ straight for about 50 meters. The park is on your right.
A Thank you very much.

e 💬 In pairs, practice the conversation in 4d. Take turns being A and B.

5 PRONUNCIATION
Sentence stress

a ▶05.18 Read and listen to B's directions in 4d. Notice the stressed words.

Go <u>straight</u> and turn <u>right</u> at the <u>corner</u>. Go <u>down</u> <u>King</u> <u>Street</u> until you come to <u>Park</u> <u>Road</u>, then turn <u>left</u>. Go <u>straight</u> for about <u>fifty</u> <u>meters</u>. The <u>park</u> is on your <u>right</u>.

b Choose the correct answer.

When we give directions, we stress … .
1 only the verbs and nouns
2 the words for direction and place
3 the little words that connect ideas

c 💬 In pairs, take turns asking for and giving directions like the conversation in 4d. Use phrases from 4 and the map in 3f. Give directions to different places.

6 SPEAKING

a ⟫ **Communication 5C** Student A go to p. 131. Student B go to p. 132.

☑ UNIT PROGRESS TEST

→ CHECK YOUR PROGRESS

You can now do the Unit Progress Test.

5D | SKILLS FOR WRITING
It isn't very exciting, but it's a nice place to live

Learn to write a description of your neighborhood

W Linking ideas with *and*, *but*, and *so*

1 SPEAKING AND LISTENING

a What makes a good neighborhood? Check (✓) four ideas.

- ☐ a lot of stores
- ☐ a soccer stadium
- ☐ no shops or cafés
- ☐ a supermarket
- ☐ a lot of restaurants
- ☐ a movie theater
- ☐ a fitness center
- ☐ a museum

b 💬 Talk about your ideas in 1a.

c ▶05.19 Lexie, Jacob, and Sara talk about what they think makes a good neighborhood. Listen and answer the questions.

1 Who likes a neighborhood that is … ?
   a new   b busy   c quiet
2 Who do you agree with?

Lexie

Sara

Jacob

d ▶05.19 Listen again. Write the places in the box next to the people who talk about them.

houses restaurants shopping mall clubs
stores cafés museum movie theater park

1 Lexie _____
2 Jacob _____
3 Sara _____

Who likes their neighborhood? Who doesn't?

e 💬 Ask and answer questions about your neighborhood.

> Are there any stores in your neighborhood?

> Yes, there are a lot.

> There's a really good café near my house.

2 READING

a Read the blog description and answer the questions.

1 What can you read about on this website?
2 What does the website want you to do?

b Read the blog post about Hannah's and Marianna's neighborhoods. Do Hannah and Marianna live in the same kind of neighborhood?

c Underline the correct answers.

1 *Hannah / Marianna* lives close to downtown.
2 *Hannah / Marianna* likes a neighborhood that isn't noisy.
3 *Hannah / Marianna* lives near a museum.
4 It's easy for *Hannah / Marianna* to eat in a restaurant.
5 There's a place where *Hannah / Marianna* can get some exercise near her home.

AROUND THE WORLD
ONLINE
TRAVEL THE WORLD WITHOUT LEAVING HOME!

Read about different neighborhoods from around the world. You can learn about real life in lots of different countries by looking at photos and reading about where people live – these are places tourists never go to!

And we want you to write about your neighborhood. Tell us all about it and what you think of it.

CLICK HERE TO ENTER A DIFFERENT WORLD.

3 WRITING SKILLS
Linking ideas with *and*, *but*, and *so*

a Underline one word in each sentence below that links two ideas.

1 There are a lot of good restaurants in my neighborhood, and my apartment's across from a really good Thai restaurant, Siam Café.
2 My neighborhood isn't very exciting, but it's a nice place to live.
3 There aren't any restaurants or bars in the area, so it's nice and quiet.

IN MY NEIGHBORHOOD

My neighborhood's about two kilometers from downtown. It's easy for me to get downtown, but everything I need is in my neighborhood, so I don't go downtown very often. It's near the art museum, and there are some beautiful old buildings here, so it's an interesting part of the city. There are a lot of good restaurants in my neighborhood, and my apartment's across from a really good Thai restaurant, Siam Café. I love their food, and it's cheap, so I eat there often.

Hannah

My neighborhood's about eight kilometers from downtown, but there's a subway station near my house, so it's easy to get there. There aren't any restaurants in the area, so it's nice and quiet. About a kilometer away there's a big shopping mall with a lot of shops. Across from it, there's a park and a fitness center. I go there three times a week to use the gym. My neighborhood isn't very exciting, but it's a nice place to live.

Marianna

b Look at the sentences in 3a and complete the rules with the words in the box.

so   and   but

1 We use _____ when we want to add an extra idea.
2 We use _____ when we want to add a different idea.
3 We use _____ when we want to add an idea that is the result of the first idea.

c Read the blog post again. Underline sentences that contain linking words.

d Put the linking words in the correct place in the sentences.

1 My neighborhood's downtown there are a lot of different stores near my house. (and)
2 I live near the university there are a lot of interesting stores in my neighborhood. (so)
3 My neighborhood's pretty busy during the day it's nice and quiet at night. (but)
4 My house is near a park there's a small river with a bridge in the park. (and)
5 My neighborhood is very friendly it's a nice place to live sometimes it's noisy in the evening. (so, but)
6 There's a popular coffee shop in my neighborhood I don't like coffee I never go there. (but, so)

4 WRITING

a Plan a description of your neighborhood. Take notes.
- where
- near
- what
- adjectives

b Write about your neighborhood. Use the blog post about Hannah's and Marianna's neighborhoods and your notes in 4a to help you. Use *and*, *but*, and *so*.

c Switch descriptions with another student and check the linking words.

d Read about other students' neighborhoods. Which one is most different from yours?

UNIT 5
Review and extension

1 GRAMMAR

a Complete the conversation with the correct form of *there is* or *there are*.

LUCAS	Can you tell me about your available room?
MRS. SMITH	¹_____ a bed, two armchairs, and a big window.
LUCAS	²_____ a desk?
MRS. SMITH	No, ³_____, but ⁴_____ a small table.
LUCAS	And ⁵_____ a private bathroom?
MRS. SMITH	No, but ⁶_____ a bathroom on the same floor.
LUCAS	I see. And ⁷_____ other students in the house?
MRS. SMITH	Yes. ⁸_____ four other students.

b Change the *marked* words to make them shorter. Use *mine, yours, his,* etc.

A Is this bag ¹*your bag*? yours
B No, it isn't ²*my bag*.

A Look, I think this is Theresa's phone.
B I know it isn't ³*our phone*, so maybe it's ⁴*her phone*. Let's ask her.

A Whose car is that?
B It's ⁵*my brother's car*. And the motorcycle's ⁶*his motorcycle*, too.

A I think that's my book.
B No, this book's ⁷*my book*. I don't know where ⁸*your book* is.

2 VOCABULARY

a Underline the correct words.

1 They live in a big *apartment / river* downtown.
2 It costs a lot to stay in this *bridge / hotel*.
3 There are a lot of good *restaurants / parks* in the main *river / square*.
4 Let's go to the *apartment / park*. We can play soccer.
5 There's only one *square / bridge* over the river.
6 The train gets in to the *park / station* at 6:30.

b Complete the sentences with things you find in a room.

1 Look in the m_____. Your face is dirty.
2 I just want to wash my hands in the s_____.
3 You can put your clean clothes in the d_____.
4 I'm tired. I'll lie on the c_____ for a bit.
5 Put your dirty clothes in the w_____ m_____.
6 Don't touch the s_____. It's hot!
7 I always keep a book on my n_____.

3 WORDPOWER Prepositions of place

a Match cafés 1–6 with a–f on the map below.

1 **Alpha Café** A busy student café <u>on</u> Newton Street, <u>next</u> to Rex Theaters. Cheap, but usually full.

2 **Café Uno** On the corner of Newton Street and Green Street. Good coffee and great cakes, but expensive.

3 **Café Express.** A small café just in front of the train station.

4 **La Roma.** A small café on Green Street, between the market and the library. They have good pasta dishes.

5 **Shane's.** At the end of Newton Street, across from the station. Popular with mothers and young children.

6 **Café Casablanca.** A Moroccan café with a nice garden. It's on a small street behind Rex Theaters.

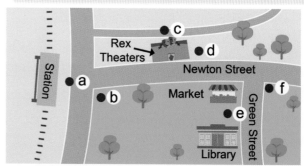

b Look at the <u>underlined</u> examples in 3a. Words like **on** and **next to** are prepositions of place that tell us where something is. <u>Underline</u> more prepositions of place in 3a.

c Add one more word to make the sentences correct.

1 The movie theater is on Market Street, next the supermarket.
2 There's an ATM the end of Orange Street.
3 I'll meet you in front the bank on Main Street.
4 There's a new bookstore the corner of New Street.

d 💬 Work in pairs. Choose four numbers on the map below. Take turns describing and guessing where they are. Use prepositions of place.

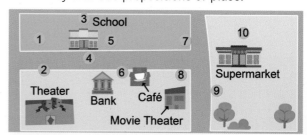

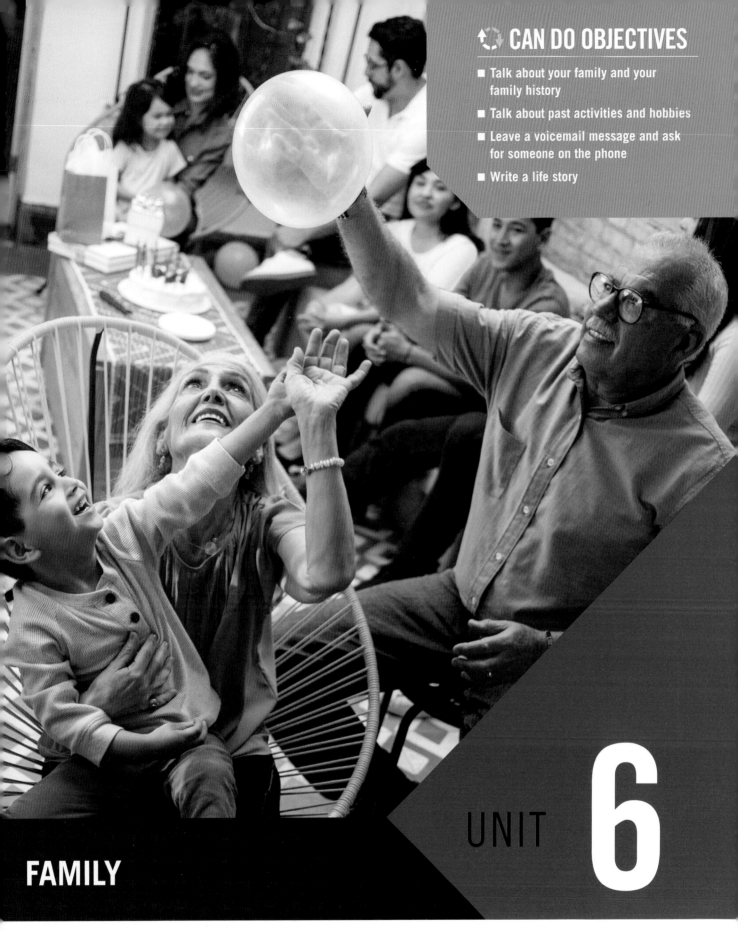

CAN DO OBJECTIVES

- Talk about your family and your family history
- Talk about past activities and hobbies
- Leave a voicemail message and ask for someone on the phone
- Write a life story

FAMILY

UNIT **6**

GETTING STARTED

a 💬🎤 Look at the picture and answer the questions.

1 Who do you think the people in this family are? Use family words you know, like "mother" and "sister."
2 Do you think they all live together in one house?
3 Choose someone in the photo. Write two questions to ask them.

b 💬🎤 Talk about a family you know well – not your own family.

1 How many people are there in the family? Who are they?
2 Who do you know the best in the family? Why?

6A | SHE WAS A DOCTOR

Learn to talk about your family and your family history

G Simple past: *be*

V Family; Years and dates

1 VOCABULARY Family

a 💬 Talk about your parents, brothers, or sisters. Think about:
- their names
- what they do
- adjectives about them

b ▶️ 06.01 Listen to Part 1. Greg talks about his family. Check (✓) the people he talks about.

- ☐ aunt
- ☐ grandparents
- ☐ uncle
- ☐ grandchildren
- ☐ sister
- ☐ granddaughter
- ☐ brother
- ☐ grandson
- ☐ grandmother
- ☐ cousin
- ☐ grandfather
- ☐ parents

c Choose words in 1b to complete Greg's family tree.

d ▶️ 06.01 Listen again and check your answers in 1c. Whose parents were born in Honduras?

e ▶️ 06.02 **Pronunciation** Listen to the letters in **bold**. Check (✓) the words that have the same sound as *but* /ʌ/.

c**ou**sin   **u**ncle   **au**nt   grandm**o**ther   grands**o**n

f Look at the family tree again. Who can say these sentences?
1. "Alice is my aunt." _Greg, Lily, Rick_
2. "Fernando's our uncle." _____
3. "Lily's our granddaughter." _____
4. "Rick, Lily, and Greg are our cousins." _____
5. "We have three grandchildren." _____

g 💬 Draw your own family tree. Show it to your partner and talk about how many people there are.

2 LISTENING

a ▶️ 06.03 Put the life events in the correct order on the timeline. Listen again and check your answers.
1. got married
2. grandfather was born
3. grandmother retired from her job
4. photographer took the picture
5. went to college
6. grandmother was born

☐ 1943   ☐ 1964   ☐ 1969
☐ 1945   ☐ 1968   ☐ 2010

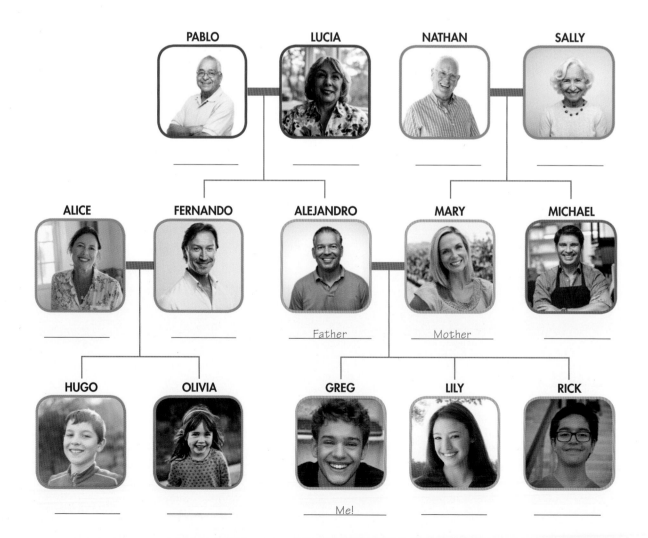

PABLO   LUCIA   NATHAN   SALLY

ALICE   FERNANDO   ALEJANDRO   MARY   MICHAEL

Father   _Mother_

HUGO   OLIVIA   GREG   LILY   RICK

_Me!_

Nathan and Sally

3 GRAMMAR Simple past: *be*

a Underline the correct words.

1 Greg's grandparents *are* / *aren't* still alive.
2 His grandmother *is* / *isn't* a doctor now.
3 His grandmother *was* / *wasn't* a doctor.
4 His grandparents *were* / *weren't* high school classmates.
5 They *were* / *weren't* friends in high school.

b Choose the correct answers to complete the rules.

1 We use *was* / *were* to talk about:	a now	b the past
2 To make a negative sentence, we add:	a *'nt*	b *n't*

c Complete the chart with *was*, *were*, *wasn't*, or *weren't*.

+	−
I ___was___ sick. She _____ a doctor.	I ___wasn't___ sick. He _____ a teacher. He was a doctor.
We ___were___ classmates. They _____ friends in college.	No, we _____ in the same class. They _____ married yet in 1960.

d ▶06.04 Listen again and complete the conversation. Which words are repeated in the question and answer?

A What about your grandfather? ¹_____ he a doctor, too?
B Yes, he ²_____.
A ³_____ they in the same class?
B No, they ⁴_____.
A When ⁵_____ she born?
B She ⁶_____ born in 1945, I think.

e ⟫ Now go to Grammar Focus 6A on p. 148.

f ▶06.06 **Pronunciation** Listen to the sentences. If *was* or *were* are stressed, underline them.

1 She was a doctor.
2 They were in school together.
3 When was she born?
4 Was she a doctor? Yes, she was.

g Complete the rules with *are* or *aren't*.

In affirmative sentences and questions, *was* and *were* _____ stressed.
In short answers, *was* and *were* _____ stressed.

h Complete the questions with the correct past forms of the verb *be*.

1 Where _____ you born?
2 Who _____ your first teacher?
3 What _____ your first school called?
4 _____ yesterday a good day for you?

i 💬 Ask and answer the questions in 3h.

4 VOCABULARY Years and dates

a ▶06.07 In Part 2, Greg talks about years and dates. Listen and answer the questions.

1 How do we say 1945?
a one thousand nine hundred and forty-five
b nineteen forty-five
c both a and b are correct
2 How do we say 2010?
a two thousand and ten
b twenty ten
c both a and b are correct
3 What do we add to 16 when we say *July 16*?

b ▶06.08 Listen and check (✓) the years you hear. Then practice saying them.

☐ 2002 ☐ 1930 ☐ 1918 ☐ 2011
☐ 2012 ☐ 1913 ☐ 1989 ☐ 2001

c ⟫ Go to Vocabulary Focus 6A on p. 165.

5 SPEAKING

a Take notes about the people in your family tree in 1g.
• When were they born?   • How old are they?
• Where do they live?   • What do they do?

b 💬 Ask and answer questions about your family trees.

6B | I PLAYED ANYTHING AND EVERYTHING

1 READING

a 💬 Ask and answer the questions.

1 Who's the man in the pictures?
2 What do you know about his company?
3 What do you know about his family life?

b 💬 The article is called "His Family Secret." What do you think the secret is? Talk about the ideas and choose one.

1 His grandfather got married four times.
2 He had a secret sister.
3 His father was a famous actor.
4 He never met his brother.

c Read the article and check your answer in 1b.

d Put the events from Steve Jobs' life in the correct order.

a ☐ Steve started a new hobby: electronics.
b ☐ His sister Mona was born.
c ☐ Steve became friends with Steve Wozniak.
d ☐ Steve's birth parents couldn't keep him.
e ☐ Steve met his sister.
f ☐ Clara and Paul Jobs became Steve's parents.
g ☐ The two Steves became very rich.
h ☐ Apple Computers began.

HIS FAMILY SECRET

His name is famous around the world, and every day millions of people use the products he made – our phones, computers, laptops, tablets, and smartwatches. We all think we know his story from magazines, newspapers, and the Internet, but how much do we really know about him?

Steve Jobs was born in San Francisco in 1955. His birth parents were university students. They decided not to keep their son, so Steve was adopted by Clara and Paul Jobs.

The Jobs family lived in Mountain View, California. This area is now known as Silicon Valley, where there are a lot of big technology companies. Steve's hobby as a child was electronics. He made simple computers with his father at the family home. In high school, he met Steve Wozniak. They both loved electronics and became good friends. In 1976, they started Apple Computers in Steve's parents' garage. They worked hard, and four years later, the company was worth $1.2 billion.

Two years after that, Steve found out about his sister for the first time. After he was adopted, his birth parents had another child, Mona, who became a famous writer. This amazing brother and sister were close friends until he died in 2011. People will continue to remember Steve when they see or use an Apple product.

2 GRAMMAR Simple past: affirmative

a Underline the simple past form of verbs 1–5 in the text.

1 work
2 start
3 live
4 decide
5 love

b Complete the rule.

To form the simple past of regular verbs add _____ or _____.

c ▶ 06.11 **Pronunciation** Listen to the infinitive and the simple past form of the verbs in 1a. Which two verbs have an extra syllable in the past?

d Complete the rule with two sounds.

-ed endings have an extra syllable /əd/ only after _____ and _____.

e ▶ 06.12 💬 Practice saying these simple past forms. Which have an extra syllable? Listen and check your answers.

- looked
- waited
- arrived
- finished
- hated
- wanted
- remembered
- needed

f Underline the simple past form of verbs 1–4 in "His Family Secret." Are these verbs regular or irregular?

1 have   2 find   3 make   4 become

g ⟫ Now go to Grammar Focus 6B on p. 148.

3 LISTENING

a Steve Jobs' hobby when he was a child was electronics. Check (✓) the hobbies you had when you were a child.

☐ reading   ☐ taking photos
☐ drawing pictures ☐ playing the guitar

Can you think of other hobbies?

b ▶ 06.14 Listen to Hannah and Charlie. What were their childhood hobbies?

c ▶ 06.14 Listen again and complete the notes about Hannah and Charlie.

	Hannah	Charlie
hobby details	basketball	cakes
parents' problem		
now		

4 VOCABULARY
Simple past irregular verbs

a Hannah and Charlie use the simple past irregular verbs in the box in their conversation. Match them with 1–9.

| went | spent | got | made | told |
| came | bought | cost | ate |

1 buy   4 go   7 make
2 eat   5 cost   8 get
3 tell   6 spend   9 come

b ⟫ Now go to Vocabulary Focus 6B on p. 165.

c 💬 Use the verbs *go, eat, buy, make,* and *get* to talk about things you did:

- last night
- yesterday
- last week
- last year

5 SPEAKING

a ▶ 06.18 Read about Becky's hobby. Complete the text with the simple past form of the verbs in the box. Listen and check your answers.

| play | buy | like | listen | have | start |

When I was young, my hobby was playing the piano. I only ¹_____ jazz, not modern or classical music. My parents ²_____ me a piano when I was eight years old, and I ³_____ lessons then. They ⁴_____ a lot of jazz CDs, and I always ⁵_____ to them. So they were happy for me to play jazz. I ⁶_____ jazz piano all the time. I still play the piano now, and jazz is still my favorite music.

b Think of a hobby you had when you were a child. Make notes. Read Becky's example in 5a to help you. Think about:

- what you did
- how your parents helped you

c 💬 Talk with a partner about your childhood hobby. Start the conversation with this question.

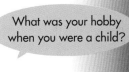

What was your hobby when you were a child?

1 LISTENING

a 💬 If you call a friend and there's no answer, what do you usually do? Say why.

- leave a message
- send them a text
- call again later

b ▶ 06.19 Listen to Part 1. Who does Sofia call?

c ▶ 06.19 Listen to Part 1 again. Are the sentences true or false?

1 Mateo answers his phone.
2 Sofia tells Mateo to call her tomorrow.

2 USEFUL LANGUAGE
Leaving a voicemail message

a Which sentences do Mateo (*M*) or Sofia (*S*) say?

1 Please leave me a message.
2 Where are you?
3 Call me back.
4 Hello ...
5 I can't answer your call right now.

b ▶ 06.19 Listen to Part 1 again and check your answers in 2a.

c ▶ 06.20 Complete the voicemail message and the caller's message with the words in the box. Listen and check.

this message it's call here back

Voicemail
Hello, ¹_____ is Alex. Sorry, I'm not ²_____ right now. Please leave a ³_____ and I'll call you later.

Caller
Hi, ⁴_____ Pam. Could you call me ⁵_____? You can ⁶_____ me at work.

d 💬 Work in pairs. Use the dialogue map to leave a message. Take turns being A and B.

A   B

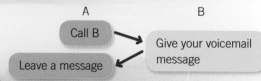

Call B → Give your voicemail message

Leave a message ←

3 LISTENING

a ▶ **06.21** Put events a–e in the order they happened. Listen to Part 2 and check your answers.

a ☐ Mateo beats his high score on a video game.
b ☐1☐ Sofia calls Mateo.
c ☐ Chris answers the phone.
d ☐ Sofia talks to Mateo.
e ☐ Sofia tells Chris her message is important.

b Complete the sentences.

1 Sofia and Mateo talk about _____.
   a how they are   c their afternoon plans
   b the weather
2 Mateo promised to drive _____ to the airport.
   a Grandma   b Sofia   c Dad
3 Dad called _____.
   a Sofia   b Mateo   c Grandma
4 _____ is picking Grandma up at the airport.
   a Dad   b Sofia   c Mateo

4 USEFUL LANGUAGE
Asking for someone on the phone

a ▶ **06.21** Look at the questions and answers. Underline the correct words. Then listen to Part 2 again and check your answers.

SOFIA Is Mateo ¹*here / there*?
CHRIS He's ²*here / there*, but he's busy right now.
SOFIA Please put him on the phone.
CHRIS He can't talk now. Can he call you ³*back / there*?

b 💬 Work in pairs. Use the dialogue map to ask for someone. Take turns being A and B.

A   B

Call Student B.
You want to speak
to another student.
→
Answer and say that
he/she isn't here.

Ask him/her to
call you back.

5 CONVERSATION SKILLS
Asking someone to wait

a Complete the conversation with the words in the box.

just   wait   minute (x2)

ROB   Can you ¹____ a ²____? He's writing an email.
MARY Sure.

ROB   Eric, it's Mary on the phone.
ERIC Oh, good. ³____ a ⁴____.

b What does *a minute* mean in the conversation?

a exactly one minute   b a short time

c 💬 Practice the conversation in 4b again. Use expressions in 5a.

6 PRONUNCIATION
Sound and spelling: *a*

a ▶ **06.22** Listen to the sound of the letter *a* in the words below.

Sound 1 /æ/	Sound 2 /ɔː/	Sound 3 /ɪ/	Sound 4 /eɪ/
th**a**nks	c**a**ll	mess**a**ge	l**a**ter

b ▶ **06.23** What sound do the letters in **bold** have in the words in the box? Add them to the sound groups in 6a. Listen and check. Listen and repeat.

t**a**lk   vill**a**ge   w**a**it   t**a**ll   b**a**ck   lugg**a**ge
voicem**a**il   s**a**me   sm**a**ll   t**a**ble   bl**a**ck

c 💬 Work in pairs. Cover the chart in 6a. Student A: say a word from 6b. Student B: say a word that has the same sound. Then switch roles.

7 SPEAKING

a ▶ **06.24** Listen and complete the phone conversation.

SUE   Hello, Melanie Wilson's office. This is Sue Parker speaking.
JOSH   Hi, Sue. ¹_____ Josh. Is Melanie there?
SUE   No, sorry. She's not ²_____ right now. She's in a meeting. Do you want to leave a ³_____?
JOSH   No, that's OK. Can she call me ⁴_____?
SUE   OK, I'll tell her.
JOSH   Thanks. She can ⁵_____ me at work.
SUE   OK. … Just a ⁶_____. I need to find a pen to write the number.
JOSH   Oh, it's OK, she has my number.

JOSH: Hello?
MELANIE Hi, Josh. ⁷_____ Melanie.
JOSH   Hi, Melanie!
MELANIE Sue says you ⁸_____.
JOSH   Yes, that's right. Do you want to meet on Friday? We can go out to dinner.
MELANIE Yes, I'd love to.

b ≫ **Communication 6C** Student A go to p. 131. Student B go to p. 132. Student C go to p. 130.

☑ UNIT PROGRESS TEST

→ **CHECK YOUR PROGRESS**

You can now do the Unit Progress Test.

6D | SKILLS FOR WRITING
Five months later, we got married

1 LISTENING AND SPEAKING

a Choose two important years in your life. Make notes about what happened in each year.

1999 – started school

b 💬🗨 Tell your partner what happened in your two important years.

c ▶06.25 The years below were important in Eva's life. What do you think happened? Match the phrases with the years. Listen and check.

a got a job as a teacher
b went to live in the U.S.
c moved to Germany
d was born
e met her husband

☐ 1992   ☐ 2005   ☐ 2014   ☐ 2017   ☐ 2019

Eva

d ▶06.25 <u>Underline</u> the correct answers. Listen again and check.

1 She was born in a *small / large* town in Colombia.
2 She went to the U.S. *alone / with her parents*.
3 She taught *young children / teenagers*.
4 She went to Germany *to get a job / to be near Niko*.

e 💬🗨 Write two more important years in your life. Tell your partner the years. Guess what happened in your partner's years.

Cartagena

66

2 READING

a Look at the timeline. Put sentences a–f about George in the correct order.

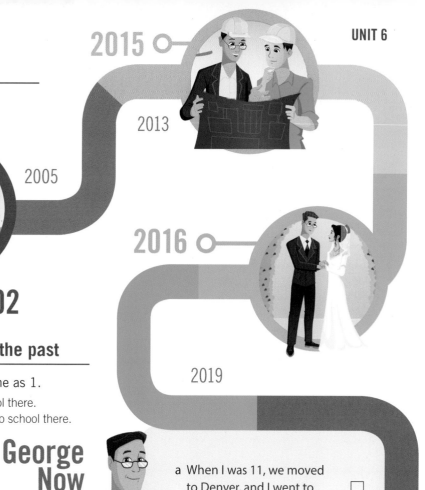

2015

2013

1998

2005

1991 2002

2016

2019

3 WRITING SKILLS Linking ideas in the past

a Complete sentence 2 so that it means the same as 1.

1 In 2002, we moved to Denver, and I went to school there.
2 _____ I was 11, we moved to Denver, and I went to school there.

b Complete the sentences with *in* or *when*.

1 I graduated from high school _____ I was 18.
2 _____ 2010, I went to college in Denver.
3 _____ I was in Australia, I worked as an engineer.

Which word (*in* or *when*) do we use … ?
a with years   b in longer sentences

George Now

c Complete the sentences that are true for you.
Write when you did each thing using *in* or *when*.

1 I started school …
2 I graduated from high school …
3 I went to college …
4 I met my wife / husband / friend …
5 I got my first job …
6 I first went on a plane …
7 I got my first phone / computer …

d Complete sentence 2 so that it means the same as 1.

1 I graduated high school in 2009. In 2010, I went to college.
2 I graduated from high school in 2009. A year _____, I went to college.

e Change the underlined expressions using a time expression + *later*.

1 I graduated from college in 2014. In 2015, I went to work in Australia.
2 I met Carolina in January 2016. In June 2016, we got married.
3 We got married in June 2016. In June 2019, we had our first child.

f Write two sentences in the past about you or someone in your family. Use *later* in the second sentence.

I came to the U.S. in January 2018. Three months later, I found a job.

g 💬🔊 Read aloud your sentences, but stop after the word *later*. Can your partner guess how they end?

I came to the U.S. in January 2018. Three months later, …

… you bought a house?

a When I was 11, we moved to Denver, and I went to school there. ☐

b In Australia, I met Carolina, and we got married a few months later. ☐

c A year later, I went to college in Denver and studied engineering. ☐

d I was born in 1991 in Omaha, Nebraska. [1]

e Then in 2015, I got a job as an engineer in Australia. ☐

f I graduated from high school in 2009, and I got a job in a bank. ☐

4 WRITING AND SPEAKING

a Think about someone in your family. Draw a timeline like George's and add notes.

b Write a life story from your notes using *he* or *she*. Don't write the name of the person or say what your relationship to the person is.

c 💬🔊 Switch life stories with another student and guess who the people are.

d Read your partner's life story again. Check how ideas are linked in the past.

UNIT 6
Review and extension

1 GRAMMAR

a Complete the conversation with the correct form of the verb *be*. Use contractions if possible.

ANNA Hi, Jenny. How [1]_____ you?
JENNY I [2]_____ fine, thanks.
ANNA [3]_____ you at the meeting yesterday?
JENNY Yes, I [4]_____, but it [5]_____ very useful.
ANNA What about Phil? [6]_____ he at the meeting?
JENNY No, he [7]_____. He [8]_____ home sick.
ANNA Oh, poor guy. [9]_____ he OK today?
JENNY Yes, I think so. He [10]_____ here today.

b Complete the text with the correct simple past form of the verbs in parentheses.

When I [1]_____ (be) a child, I [2]_____ (want) to be a truck driver. I [3]_____ (love) big trucks, and I [4]_____ (have) a lot of toy trucks. But when I [5]_____ (be) about twelve years old, I [6]_____ (decide) that trucks were boring. After high school, I [7]_____ (study) business in college, but I [8]_____ (find) that boring, too. Now I'm a chef and I love it.

c Complete the sentences with the simple present or the simple past form of the verbs in parentheses.

1 Last night we _____ (stay) home, and my husband _____ (cook) an amazing dinner.
2 I _____ (go) to the country with my family last weekend. We _____ (have) a really nice time together.
3 My sister _____ (play) volleyball on Tuesday nights. She usually _____ (get) home at about 7:30 p.m., but tonight she _____ (get) back at 8:15 p.m.
4 My brother and I _____ (spend) a lot of time together when we _____ (be) children, but now we almost never _____ (see) each other.

2 VOCABULARY

a Complete the text with the correct family words.

Peter and Barbara are my father's parents, so they are my [1]_____. I'm very close to my [2]_____ Barbara, and to my [3]_____ Peter, too. My father has only one sister, Helen, and she married Jonathan. My mother doesn't have any brothers or sisters, so Helen is my only [4]_____ and Jonathan is my only [5]_____. They have three children, so I have three [6]_____.

b Write the date in words.

12/25/1982 – *December twenty-fifth, nineteen eighty-two*

1 10/19/2014   4 4/22/2008
2 6/12/1985   5 8/31/2020
3 9/3/1990   6 1/9/2012

3 WORDPOWER *go*

a Read the conversation and answer the questions.

SARAH I need to [1]**go home** now.
VIV I can drive you.
SARAH No, no. I can [2]**go by** bus.
VIV Are you sure?
SARAH Yes, I need to [3]**go shopping** on the way home. The supermarket is next to the bus stop.
VIV Do you want to [4]**go out** to a restaurant later on?
SARAH Yes, that'd be nice.
VIV OK. See you later.

1 Who has a car?
2 What plans do Sarah and Viv have for later on?

b Match the phrases in **bold** in 3a with meanings a–d.

a travel by
b leave and return to where I live
c buy some things
d leave home and do something fun

c Match 1–4 with a–d to make more phrases with *go*.

1 go to   a train
2 go by   b to lunch
3 go   c a party
4 go out   d swimming

d Correct the mistakes in the sentences.

1 They want to go to home now.
2 I need to go for shopping in town this afternoon.
3 I'd like to go the movies this evening.
4 He usually goes to work for bus.

e Write sentences about your life using phrases with *go*.

1 every day / usually / go home
  Every day I usually go home at 5:30 p.m.
2 each week / go shopping
3 often go / downtown by
4 this evening / would like / go out to

f 💬 Tell a partner your sentences in 3e. How similar are you?

⟳ REVIEW YOUR PROGRESS

How well did you do in this unit? Write 3, 2, or 1 for each objective.
3 = very well   2 = well   1 = not so well

I CAN ...	
talk about my family and my family history	☐
talk about past activities and hobbies	☐
leave a voicemail message and ask for someone on the phone	☐
write a life story	☐

Phonemic symbols

Vowel sounds

/ə/	/æ/	/ʊ/	/ɑ/	/ɪ/	/i/	/e/	/ʌ/	/ɜ/	/u/	/ɔ/
breakf**a**st	m**a**n	p**u**t	g**o**t	ch**i**p	happ**y**	m**e**n	**u**p	sh**ir**t	wh**o**	w**a**lk

Diphthongs (two vowel sounds)

/eə/	/ɪə/	/ɔɪ/	/aɪ/	/eɪ/	/oʊ/	/aʊ/
h**air**	n**ear**	b**oy**	n**i**ne	**ei**ght	wind**ow**	n**ow**

Consonants

/p/	/b/	/f/	/v/	/t/	/d/	/k/	/g/
picnic	**b**ook	**f**ace	**v**ery	**t**ime	**d**og	**c**old	**g**o
/θ/	/ð/	/tʃ/	/dʒ/	/s/	/z/	/ʃ/	/ʒ/
think	**th**e	**ch**air	**j**ob	**s**ea	**z**oo	**sh**oe	televi**si**on
/m/	/n/	/s/	/h/	/l/	/r/	/w/	/j/
me	**n**ow	si**ng**	**h**ot	**l**ate	**r**ed	**w**ent	**y**es

Irregular verbs

Infinitive	Simple past		Infinitive	Simple past
be	was		meet	met
begin	began		pay	paid
buy	bought		put	put
catch	caught		read	read
choose	chose		ride	rode
come	came		run	ran
do	did		say	said
drink	drank		see	saw
drive	drove		sell	sold
eat	ate		send	sent
feel	felt		sing	sang
find	found		sit	sat
fly	flew		sleep	slept
forget	forgot		speak	spoke
get	got		swim	swam
give	gave		take	took
go	went		teach	taught
grow up	grew up		tell	told
have	had		think	thought
hear	heard		understand	understood
know	knew		wake up	woke up
leave	left		wear	wore
lose	lost		write	wrote

COMMUNICATION PLUS

1A STUDENT A

a Read this social media profile. Answer Student B's questions about Roberto.

 Hi! My name's Roberto. I'm from Cancún. It's a nice city by the sea in southern Mexico. I'm a student at Maryland University in the U.S.

b Ask Student B your questions. Write their answers.

1 What's her name? _____Lora_____
2 What's her nationality? _____
3 What's her hometown? _____
4 Where is she now? _____

c ⋙ Now go back to p. 11.

2A STUDENT A

a Read about the job. Complete the sentences with the correct forms of the verbs.

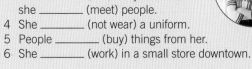

Salesperson
1 She _____ (start) work at 8:00 a.m.
2 She _____ (not work) on Sunday.
3 She _____ (like) her job because she _____ (meet) people.
4 She _____ (not wear) a uniform.
5 People _____ (buy) things from her.
6 She _____ (work) in a small store downtown.

b Read your sentences out loud. Student B tries to guess the job after each sentence.

c Listen to Student B's sentences and guess the job.

d ⋙ Now go back to p. 21.

6C STUDENT C

a **Conversation 1.** Read your first card. Then listen to Student B and reply.

 ①
- You return home. Student B has a message for you from Student A.
- Call Student A back. Have a conversation.

b **Conversation 2.** Now look at your second card. Start the conversation with Student B.

②
- Student B calls and you answer the phone.
- He/She wants to speak to Student A, who isn't there. Take a message.
- Student A returns. Give him/her Student B's message.

c **Conversation 3.** Now look at your third card. Think about what you want to say. Then call Student B.

③
- Think of a reason to call Student B.
- You call Student B, but he/she isn't there. Leave a message with Student A.
- Student B calls you back. Have a conversation.

4A STUDENT A

a **Conversation 1.** Look at the picture. Answer Student B's questions about what's at your stall. Look at the examples.

Do you have any apples at your stall?

I'd like some onions, please.

Yes, I do.

I'm sorry, I don't have any onions.

b **Conversation 2.** You want to buy food to cook dinner. You visit Student B's market stall. Ask about the things in the box. Look at the examples.

chicken	eggs	one lemon	fruit	tomatoes	mushrooms
cheese	pears	vegetables	bread	one onion	apples

Do you have any eggs at your stall?

I'd like some mushrooms, please.

2C STUDENT A

a **Conversation 1.** Read your first card. Think about what you want to say. Then start the conversation with Student B.

 ①
You're at Student B's home for the weekend. You'd like to do the following things:
- have something to eat
- use your friend's computer
- watch TV

b **Conversation 2.** Now look at your second card. Listen to Student B and reply.

 ②
Student B's at your home for the weekend. You're good friends, but you don't like it when other people use your things, especially your new phone.

5A STUDENT A

a Look at your picture. Student B has a similar picture. Ask and answer questions to find six differences.

Is there a park in your picture?

Yes, there is. / No, there isn't.

b ≫ Now go back to p. 51.

1C STUDENT A

a **Conversation 1.** Read your first card. Think about what you want to say. Then start the conversation with Student B.

① You want to ask about beginner guitar lessons.
Talk to the receptionist at the music school.
- Say what you would like to do.
- Ask when the first lesson is.
- Ask where the lesson is.
- Sign up for lessons.

b **Conversation 2.** Now look at your second card. Listen to Student B and reply.

② You're a receptionist in a language school. Here's some information about an English course:
- *Time:* 6:20 p.m. next Tuesday
- *Place:* Room 12
- To sign a student up, you need the student's name.

6C STUDENT A

a **Conversation 1.** Read your first card. Think about what you want to say. Then call Student C.

① • Think of a reason to call Student C.
- You call Student C but he/she isn't there. Leave a message with Student B.
- Student C calls you back. Have a conversation.

b **Conversation 2.** Now look at your second card. Listen to Student C and reply.

② • You return home. Student C has a message for you from Student B.
- Call Student B back. Have a conversation.

c **Conversation 3.** Now look at your third card. Start the conversation with Student C.

③ • Student C calls and you answer the phone.
- He/She wants to speak to Student B, who isn't there. Take a message.
- Student B returns. Give him/her Student C's message.

4B SPEAKING 5C

Healthy food

Every day you can eat these food quantities:

bread – 4 slices	rice or pasta – 2 cups
vegetables – 5 pieces	fruit – 2 pieces
cheese – 2 pieces	meat/fish – 1 piece

5C STUDENT A

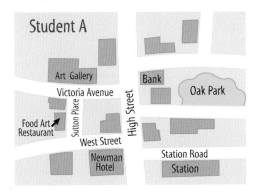

a **Conversation 1.** Read your first card. Think about what you want to say. Then start the conversation with Student B.

① You're at the station with your friend, Student B. The map on your phone isn't clear. You need to go to:
- the supermarket   • Dash Café

Student B's map is clear. Ask him/her how to get to these places. Someone told you Dash Café is on James Street, but you're not sure.

b **Conversation 2.** Now look at your second card. Think about what you want to say. Then listen to Student B and reply.

② You're at the station with your friend, Student B. The map on his/her phone isn't clear. You want to go to:
- the art gallery   • Food Art Restaurant

Use your map to tell Student B how to get there. A lot of people think that Food Art Restaurant is on the corner of Sutton Place and West Street, but that isn't correct.

5C STUDENT B

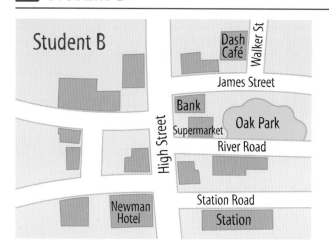

Student B

Dash Café — Walker St — James Street — Bank — Supermarket — Oak Park — High Street — River Road — Newman Hotel — Station Road — Station

a Conversation 1. Read your first card. Think about what you want to say. Then listen to Student A and reply.

1
You're at the station with your friend, Student A. The map on his/her phone isn't clear. You need to go to:
- the supermarket • Dash Café

Use your map to tell Student A how to get there. A lot of people think that Dash Café is on James Street, but that isn't correct.

b Conversation 2. Now look at your second card. Think about what you want to say. Then start the conversation with Student A.

2
You're at the station with your friend, Student A. The map on your phone isn't clear. You want to go to:
- the art gallery • Food Art Restaurant

Student A's map is clear. Ask him/her how to get to these places. Someone told you that Food Art Restaurant is on the corner of Sutton Place and West Street, but you're not sure.

6C STUDENT B

a Conversation 1. Read your first card. Start the conversation with Student A.

1
- Student A calls and you answer the phone.
- He/She wants to speak to Student C, who isn't there. Take a message.
- Student C returns. Give him/her Student A's message.

b Conversation 2. Now look at your second card. Think about what you want to say. Then call Student A.

2
- Think of a reason to call Student A.
- You call Student A, but he/she isn't there. Leave a message with Student C.
- Student A calls you back. Have a conversation.

c Conversation 3. Now look at your third card. Listen to Student A and reply.

3
- You return home. Student A has a message for you from Student B.
- Call Student C back. Have a conversation.

3C STUDENT B

a Conversation 1. Read your first card. Listen to Student A and reply.

1
You aren't free this Saturday because you work on the weekends. You'd like to go out to the movies on Friday.

b Conversation 2. Now look at your second card. Think about what you want to say. Then start the conversation with Student A.

2
You want to meet Student A for coffee. You think next Friday after work/school is a good time. Decide the following and invite Student A:
- where to have coffee
- what time
- something to do after

c ≫ Now go back to 5c on p. 35.

5A STUDENT B

a Look at your picture. Student A has a similar picture. Ask and answer questions to find six differences.

Is there a bridge in your picture?

Yes, there is. / No, there isn't.

b ≫ Now go back to p. 51.

1A STUDENT B

a Read this social media profile. Answer Student A's questions about Lora.

 Hi, my name's Lora. I'm from Berlin, Germany, but now I'm in England with my family. I'm a teacher in London.

b Ask Student A your questions. Write their answers.
1 What's his name? _____Roberto_____
2 What's his nationality? _____
3 What's his hometown? _____
4 Where is he now? _____

c Now go back to p. 11.

2A STUDENT B

a Read about the job. Complete the sentences with the correct forms of the verbs.

Nurse
1 He sometimes _____ (work) at night.
2 He _____ (not make) a lot of money.
3 He _____ (wear) a uniform at work.
4 He _____ (like) his job because he _____ (help) people.
5 He _____ (give) people medicine.
6 He _____ (work) in a big hospital downtown.

b Listen to Student A's sentences and guess the job.

c Read your sentences out loud. Student A tries to guess the job after each sentence.

d Now go back to p. 21.

1C STUDENT B

a **Conversation 1.** Read your first card. Think about what you want to say. Listen to Student A and reply.

1 You're a receptionist at a music school. Here is some information about beginner guitar lessons:
- *Time*: 6:30 p.m. next Thursday
- *Place*: Room 2
- To sign a student up, you need the student's full name.

b **Conversation 2.** Now look at your second card. Think about what you want to say. Then start the conversation with Student A.

2 You want to ask about English classes. Talk to the receptionist at the language school.
- Say what you would like to do.
- Ask when the first class is.
- Ask where the class is.
- Sign up for the class.

4A STUDENT B

a **Conversation 1.** You want to buy food to cook dinner. You visit Student A's market stall. Ask about the things in the box. Look at the examples.

steak one lemon beans fruit tomatoes mushrooms
cheese pears vegetables bread one onion apples

Do you have any apples at your stall?

I'd like some pears, please.

b **Conversation 2.** Look at the picture. Answer Student A's questions about what's at your stall. Look at the examples.

Do you have any eggs at your stall?

Yes, I do.

I'd like some mushrooms, please.

I'm sorry, I don't have any mushrooms.

2C STUDENT B

a **Conversation 1.** Read your first card. Think about what you want to say. Listen to Student A and reply.

1 Student A's at your home for the weekend. You're good friends, but you don't like it when other people use your things, especially your computer.

b **Conversation 2.** Now look at your second card. Think about what you want to say. Then start the conversation with Student A.

2 You're at Student A's home for the weekend. You'd like to do the following things:
- have something to drink
- use your friend's phone
- take a shower

GRAMMAR FOCUS

1A *be:* affirmative and negative

▶ 01.07

Affirmative (+)	
Full form	**Contraction**
I **am** a student.	I**'m** a student.
You **are** a good cook.	You**'re** a good cook.
He **is** my friend.	He**'s** my friend.
She **is** Spanish.	She**'s** Spanish.
It **is** sunny.	It**'s** sunny.
We **are** sisters.	We**'re** sisters.
They **are** from Japan.	They**'re** from Japan.

Negative (–)		
Full form	**Contractions**	
I **am not** a teacher.	I**'m not** a teacher.	
You **are not** French.	You**'re not** French.	You **aren't** French.
He **is not** Brazilian.	He**'s not** Brazilian.	He **isn't** Brazilian.
She **is not** my friend.	She**'s not** my friend.	She **isn't** my friend.
It **is not** sunny.	It**'s not** sunny.	It **isn't** sunny.
We **are not** sisters.	We**'re not** sisters.	We **aren't** sisters.
They **are not** students.	They**'re not** students.	They **aren't** students.

Remember to use the verb *be* to give information with a noun, adjective, preposition, or adverb.
My name**'s Hamid**. (NOT ~~My name Hamid.~~)
My teacher **is nice**. (NOT ~~My teacher nice.~~)
I**'m from China**. (NOT ~~I from China.~~)
We **are here**. (NOT ~~We here.~~)
Always use a noun or a pronoun before affirmative and negative *be*:
He**'s** my teacher. (NOT ~~Is my teacher.~~)
They**'re** Brazilian. (NOT ~~Are Brazilian.~~)

Hi! No, I'm not at home. We're on vacation in Seattle. It's a beautiful city, but it's not very warm.

◯ Tip
you is the same when we talk to one person or two or more people.
You're a good cook. = one person
You're good cooks. = two or more people

We use contractions to help us speak quickly. In contractions, the apostrophe (') shows a letter is missing:
You **are not** old. ➔ You**'re not** old. / You **aren't** old.
There are two different contractions for *is not* and *are not*.
is not ➔ isn't / 's not   He **isn't** = He**'s not**
are not ➔ aren't / 're not   We **aren't** = We**'re not**

◯ Tip
We can use *'s* after one name, but we don't use *'re* after two names:
Tom is my friend. ➔ **Tom's** my friend.
Tom and Jo are my friends. (NOT Tom and ~~Jo're~~ my friends.)

1B *be:* questions and short answers

In questions with the verb *be*, we change the word order:
They are Canadian. ➔ **Are they** Canadian?
He is from San José. ➔ **Is he** from San José?

▶ 01.12

Yes/No questions		Short answers	
Are you	ready?	Yes, No,	I **am**. I**'m not**.
Am I	late?	Yes, No,	you **are**. you**'re not**. / you **aren't**.
Is it	cold?	Yes, No,	it **is**. it**'s not**. / it **isn't**.

In *Wh-* questions, we use a question word before *be*.
Where are you from?
What is your name?

◯ Tip
With affirmative short answers, we don't use contractions:
Yes, I **am**. Yes, he **is**. Yes, we **are**.
(NOT ~~Yes, I'm. Yes, he's. Yes, we're.~~)

◯ Tip
We can use the contraction of *is* with question words:
What is your name? ➔ **What's** your name?
Where is he from? ➔ **Where's** he from?

1A *be:* affirmative and negative

a Write the correct form of *be* (*am/is/are*) in these sentences.

1 We _____are_____ very happy.
2 My father _____ a taxi driver.
3 My parents _____ not old.
4 Carl and Michael _____ brothers.
5 I _____ not a good driver.
6 She _____ at work today.
7 Asheville _____ not a big city.
8 Our cats _____ hungry.

b Write the sentence again with affirmative and negative contractions. More than one negative contraction may be possible.

1 She is Brazilian.
   _____She's Brazilian._____
   _____She's not Brazilian._____
2 It is a beautiful city.
   _____
   _____
3 We are from Los Angeles.
   _____
   _____
4 They are at a party.
   _____
   _____
5 I am tired.
   _____
   _____
6 You are right.
   _____
   _____

c Complete the sentences with the correct affirmative (+) or negative (−) form of *be*. Use contractions if possible.

1 We _____'re_____ (+) at a concert.
2 She _____'s not_____ (−) Japanese.
3 I _____ (+) from Mexico City.
4 He _____ (−) home.
5 It _____ (+) a big hotel.
6 Valentina and Andre _____ (−) friends.
7 My city _____ (+) very beautiful.
8 Hi, my name _____ (+) Michael.
9 My parents _____ (−) at the game.
10 You _____ (+) very nice.

d Write the correct sentences.

1 ~~Spanish~~ → French
   She's Spanish. *She's not / She isn't Spanish. She's French.*
2 ~~a doctor~~ → a student
   He's a doctor. _____
3 ~~brothers~~ → friends
   They're my brothers. _____
4 ~~London~~ → Toronto
   We're from London. _____
5 ~~good cook~~ → very bad cook
   I'm a good cook. _____

e ≫ Now go back to p. 11.

1B *be:* questions and short answers

a Put the words in the correct order to make questions.

1 her / what / name / 's ?   _____What's her name?_____
2 from / are / you / where ?   _____
3 American / are / you ?   _____
4 she / popular / is ?   _____
5 names / are / what / your ?   _____
6 friends / you / are ?   _____
7 is / cold / it / very ?   _____
8 from / he / is / Chile ?   _____

b Match questions 1–7 with short answers a–g.

1 [d] Is she Italian?
2 [ ] Are you teachers?
3 [ ] Are Robert and Helen here today?
4 [ ] Is it a beautiful city?
5 [ ] Am I late?
6 [ ] Is he on vacation?
7 [ ] Are you from the U.S.?

a No, he's not.
b No, they're not.
c No, you're not.
d Yes, she is.
e No, I'm not.
f Yes, we are.
g Yes, it is.

c Complete the conversations with the correct form of *be*. Use contractions if possible.

1 **A** Hi, I _'m_ Manuel.
   B Hi, Manuel. Where _____ you from?
   A I _____ from Lima, Peru.

2 **A** See that soccer player? What _____ his name?
   B He _____ Philip Lahm.
   A Where _____ he from?
   B He _____ from Germany.

3 **A** Excuse me, where _____ you from?
   B We _____ from Japan. We _____ here for the World Cup.

4 **A** Hi, my name _____ Alice, and this _____ my sister, Marta.
   B Hi, Alice. Hi, Marta. _____ you from England?
   A No, we _____. We _____ American. We _____ from New York.
   B Oh really? My cousins _____ from New York.

d ≫ Now go back to p. 13.

2A Simple present: affirmative and negative

We use the simple present to talk about things that are generally true in daily life:

- habits and routines
  I **drive** to work every morning.　　My sister **doesn't eat** breakfast.
- facts and feelings
  They **have** a fast car.　　The children **don't like** coffee.

▶ 02.04

	+		–	
I / you / we / they	I	**work**.	We **don't**	**work**.
he / she / it	She	**works**.	It **doesn't**	**work**.

SPELLING: verb + -s

most verbs → add -s	start → start**s** work → work**s** play → play**s**
verb ends in consonant + -y → change -y to -i then add -es	try → tr**ies** study → stud**ies**
verb ends in -sh, -ch, -x, -ss → add -es	wa**sh** → wash**es** cat**ch** → catch**es**

💡 **Tip**

Don't add -s to the verb in negative sentences:
He doesn't **work** hard. (NOT ~~He doesn't works hard.~~)

It's not fair. I work really hard, but I don't make much money. He doesn't work hard at all, and he makes millions.

2B Simple present: questions and short answers

How many hours a day do you study?

Wow! So do you always get good grades?

About 12.

No, I don't. I usually fall asleep in the middle of my exams.

▶ 02.11

	Yes/No questions		Short answers	
I / you / we / they	**Do** you	**study**?	Yes, No,	I **do**. I **don't**.
he / she / it	**Does** she	**work**?	Yes, No,	she **does**. she **doesn't**.

	Wh- questions		
I / you / we / they	Where	do you	**work**?
he / she / it	Where	does she	**work**?

💡 **Tip**

Don't add -s to the verb in questions:
Does he **work** hard? (NOT ~~Does he works hard?~~)

2A Simple present: affirmative and negative

a Write the -s form of each verb.

1 fly _____flies_____
2 finish _____
3 relax _____
4 buy _____
5 want _____
6 miss _____
7 say _____
8 teach _____
9 worry _____
10 watch _____

b Complete the sentences with the correct simple present form of the verb in parentheses. The verbs are all affirmative.

1 I ____work____ (work) in an office. I _____ (start) work at 9 o'clock.
2 Lisa _____ (finish) school at 5 o'clock every day. She _____ (do) her homework on the bus.
3 Phil _____ (go) to work by train. The train _____ (leave) at 8:35 a.m.
4 Marta _____ (watch) TV in the evening. She _____ (try) to go to bed before eleven.
5 My parents _____ (get) up very early. My father _____ (make) their breakfast.
6 My brother _____ (have) a fast car. He _____ (love) it.
7 We _____ (study) English after work. We _____ (enjoy) our classes.

c Complete the sentences with the correct simple present form of the verb in parentheses.

1 Allan ___doesn't like___ (not like) his job.
2 My parents _____ (not drive) fast.
3 I _____ (not cook) at home.
4 She _____ (not have) a car.
5 We _____ (not worry) about work.
6 The bus _____ (not go) to my house.
7 You _____ (not do) the housework.

d Correct one mistake in each sentence.

1 I ~~studies~~ every evening. ____study____
2 Eva don't work in a hospital. _____
3 My brother gos to college. _____
4 Tom haves a very big house. _____
5 We no like this book. _____
6 I am love animals. _____

e ≫ Now go back to p. 21.

2B Simple present: questions and short answers

a Put the words in order to complete the questions.

1 like / she / does
_____Does she like_____ this class?
2 you / do / go
_____ shopping on weekends?
3 want / does / he
_____ a new computer?
4 where / you / play / do
_____ soccer?
5 they / what / do / wear
_____ to school?
6 they / lunch / what time / do / have
_____?

b Complete the sentences with do, does, don't, or doesn't.

1 What _____do_____ you do in your free time?
2 _____ Anne study hard for exams?
3 Yes, she _____. She studies very hard.
4 _____ students at your school have a lot of exams?
5 No, they _____. They just have one big exam at the end of the year.
6 Where _____ you study?
7 _____ Patrick listen to music while he studies?
8 No, he _____. He prefers to study quietly.

c Use the words in parentheses to write complete simple present questions.

1 **A** Where ___do you live___? (you / live)
  B I live in Alabama.
2 **A** What _____? (she / study)
  B French and Italian.
3 **A** What time _____? (the store / open)
  B At 10:00 a.m.
4 **A** What _____ for lunch? (you / want)
  B I want a sandwich.
5 **A** Where _____? (the bus / go)
  B The bus goes downtown.
6 **A** How many times a week _____? (you / go to the gym)
  B We go to the gym every day.
7 **A** How many hours a day _____? (they / work)
  B They work seven hours a day.

d ≫ Now go back to p. 23.

3A Position of adverbs of frequency

We often use adverbs of frequency with the simple present. Adverbs of frequency tell us how often something happens.

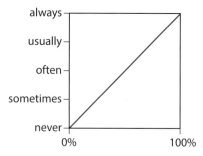

Adverbs of frequency go <u>after</u> the verb *be*.
I'**m never** late.
She **isn't always** happy.
Are they **usually** at home?

Adverbs of frequency usually go <u>before</u> other main verbs.
I **always arrive** at 8:45 a.m.
I **never** call my friends. I **always** text them.

In negatives, the adverbs go <u>between</u> *don't/doesn't* and the main verb.
I **don't usually get** up early.

Sometimes, usually, and *often* can go before the verb or at the beginning or end of a sentence.
Sometimes we go dancing on Saturdays.
My brother cooks for me **often**.

We can ask questions with *How often*:
How often do you go to English class?
How often is the bus late?

▶ 03.01

Statements with the verb *be*
I'**m sometimes** late for work.
I'**m always** tired.

Statements with other verbs
I **often play** tennis in the morning.
I **usually go** shopping in the afternoon.
I **never do** any work in the evening.

Questions
How often do you go to the movies?
When do you **usually** see your friends?

I **often play** tennis in the morning.

I **usually go** shopping in the afternoon.

I **never do** any work in the evening. I'**m always** tired.

3B *do, go,* and *have*

▶ 03.10

We can use *do, go,* and *have* to talk about actions:
They **do** a lot of homework.
Do you **do** your homework every day?
I **go** to the movies on Saturdays.
You **go** to school by bus.
Do you **have** dinner at 7:00 p.m.?
He **has** breakfast at 8:30 a.m.

We can also use *have* to talk about possessions and appearance:
I **have** a new phone.
She **has** brown eyes.

Be careful with the verbs *do, go,* and *have* after singular nouns and he/she/it:
do ➔ **does**   go ➔ **goes**   have ➔ **has**
He **does** his homework every evening.
The train **goes** to Boston.
She **has** a fast car.

	he / she / it
do	does
go	goes
have	has

> **Tip**
> What **does** she **do** on Sundays? (NOT ~~What **does** she on Sundays?~~)
> She **does** her shopping online. (NOT ~~She **dos** her shopping online.~~)

I have a great new phone. It has a virtual assistant, an excellent camera, and all the latest apps. It also has a great GPS, so I never get lost.

Do you have it with you?

No, it's at home.

3A Position of adverbs of frequency

a Put the adverbs in parentheses in the correct places in each sentence. Use them in the order given.

      never

1 I ⌄miss a visit to my parents on the weekends – I go and see them. (~~never~~, always)

2 I'm late for work, but my boss gets angry. (sometimes, never)

3 He comes here for coffee at 10 o'clock – he's late. (usually, never)

4 We have lunch together and talk. It's good to see him. (often, always)

5 They're away on vacation – they're at home. (never, always)

c Put the words in the correct order to make questions.

1 often / how / movies / do / you / to / go / the ?
      How often do you go to the movies?

2 to work / do / walk / you / usually ?
_____

3 always / are / tired / you / why ?
_____

4 you / where / usually / on weekends / go / do ?
_____

5 soccer / do / how / they / play / often ?
_____

6 often / is / late / for work / he ?
_____

7 me / you / never / do / write / to / why ?
_____

d ≫ Now go back to p. 30.

b Write sentences using the information in the chart and adverbs of frequency. always = ✓✓✓✓✓, never = ✗✗✗✗✗

	Monday	Tuesday	Wednesday	Thursday	Friday
Paul / have breakfast	✓	✓	✗	✓	✓
My parents / eat in a restaurant	✗	✓	✓	✗	✗
I / play tennis	✓	✗	✓	✗	✓
Natasha / late for work	✗	✗	✗	✗	✗
We / watch TV in the evening	✓	✓	✓	✓	✓

1 _____ *Paul usually has breakfast.* _____
2 _____
3 _____

4 _____
5 _____

3B do, go, and have

a Correct one mistake in each sentence.

1 My brother ~~have~~ a new laptop.
      My brother has a new laptop.

2 Does your sister has a car?
_____

3 Where does they go after class?
_____

4 She gos to the store on weekends.
_____

5 Does John his shopping online?
_____

6 My brother don't do his homework on his tablet.
_____

b Use the words to write questions and short answers.

1 you / have / a smartwatch
      Do you have a smartwatch? No, I don't.

2 your teacher / go / to the movies
      Does your teacher go to the movies? Yes, he does.

3 your mom / have / a digital camera
                No, she

4 your grandparents / do / yoga
                No,

5 you / go / to the library every day
                Yes,

6 your sister / do / her shopping online
                Yes,

c Complete the conversations with the correct form of the verb *do*, *go*, or *have*. Choose the correct verb.

1 **TOM**   [1] *Does your son have a tablet?*

   EMILY No, he [2] *doesn't have* a tablet, but he [3]_____ a laptop.

2 **RACHEL** Where [4]_____ you _____ on Fridays after work?

   LAURA I sometimes [5]_____ to the movies or to my friend's house.

3 **DAN** What [6]_____ Maria _____ after work?

   RAUL She often [7]_____ yoga, but she sometimes [8]_____ out with her friends.

4 **MATT** [9]_____ you [10]_____ a lot of good games on your smartphone?

   ALICIA No, I [11]_____ many games, but my sister [12]_____ a lot of great games on her phone. She plays them all the time!

5 **KYOKO** [13]_____ you _____ your homework on the bus?

   PAUL No, I [14]_____ it in the library. They always [15]_____ the Internet!

4A Count and noncount nouns: *a / an*, *some / any*

Count and noncount nouns

We <u>can</u> count some things (e.g., *one lemon, eight grapes*). These things (e.g., *lemon, grape*) are **count** nouns. They can be singular (e.g., *lemon*) or plural (e.g., *lemons*).

We <u>can't</u> count some things (e.g., *cheese* NOT ~~one cheese~~; *pasta* NOT ~~two pastas~~). These things (e.g., *cheese, pasta*) are **noncount** nouns. They can only be singular (e.g., *cheese*), not plural (~~cheeses~~).

a / an

We use *a/an* with singular nouns. *a/an* means *one*. We can't use them with plurals or noncount nouns.
We use *a* before a consonant sound:
a lemon, **a p**otato
We use *an* before a vowel sound (*a, e, i, o, u*):
an onion, **an e**gg

BUY FRUIT HERE
FRUIT BEST FRUIT FRESH FRUIT LOCAL FRUIT

Hello. Do you have any fruit?

some / any

We use *some/any* with plural and noncount nouns. We use *some/any* when we do not need to say the exact amount.
We use *some* in affirmative sentences:
I'd like **some** potatoes.
We use *any* in negative sentences and questions:
We don't have **any** potatoes.
Do you have **any** potatoes?

▶ 04.08

Count	singular	**a/an** *I have **a lemon**.* *I don't need **an onion**.*
	plural	**some/any** *We'd like **some grapes**.* *We don't want **any potatoes**.*
Noncount		**some/any** *They have **some pasta**.* *Do you want **any cheese**?*

These common nouns are noncount:

money   music   hair   furniture   fruit   water   cheese *butter   bread   rice   meat   chicken* = meat   *fish* = meat

4B Quantifiers: *much, many, a lot of*

How much? / How many?

We use *How much? / How many?* to ask about quantities.

▶ 04.14

We use *How many?* with count nouns:
How many eggs do we have?
We use *How much?* with noncount nouns:
How much milk do we have?
When we ask about a price, we can just ask *How much?*
How much does it cost?

Large and small quantities

▶ 04.15

	Count	Noncount
Large quantity	**a lot of** *I buy **a lot of grapes**.*	**a lot of** *I cook **a lot of pasta**.*
Medium quantity	**quite a few** *I eat **quite a few grapes**.*	**quite a bit of** *I eat **quite a bit of pasta**.*
Small quantity	**a few** *I eat **a few grapes** every evening.*	**a little** *I have **a little pasta**.*
	not many *We don't have **many grapes**.*	**not much** *I don't have **much pasta**.*
One	**a/an** *Would you like **a grape**?*	–
Zero quantity	**not any** *We don't have **any grapes**.*	**not any** *I don't have **any pasta**.*

a lot of / much / many

We use *a lot of / much / many* to talk about large quantities.
We use *a lot of* in affirmative sentences:
I need **a lot of** potatoes.
We often use *much/many* in negative sentences and questions:
We don't have **many** potatoes.
I don't eat **much** chocolate.
Do you have **many** potatoes?
Do you eat **much** chocolate?

> **Tip**
>
> Only use *a lot of* before a noun (e.g., *chocolate*) or a pronoun (e.g., *it*). Use *a lot* at the end of a sentence.
> *I eat **a lot of chocolate**.*
> *I eat **a lot of it**.*
> *I eat **a lot**. (NOT ~~I eat a lot of.~~)*

I don't eat **much chocolate** – just **a little** after every meal.

4A Count and noncount nouns: *a / an, some / any*

a Are these count (*C*) or noncount (*N*) nouns?

1 bread ___N___
2 carrot _____
3 cheese _____
4 chocolate _____
5 fruit _____

6 furniture _____
7 lemon _____
8 money _____
9 egg _____
10 meat _____

b Complete the conversation between a customer and a salesperson with *a, an, some,* or *any*.

CUSTOMER Hello, do you have ¹___any___ fruit?
SALESPERSON Yes, of course. This is ²_____ market and I sell fruit.
CUSTOMER Oh, good. I'd like ³_____ grapes, please.
SALESPERSON Oh, sorry, we don't have ⁴_____ grapes.
CUSTOMER Really? OK, I'd like ⁵_____ orange.
SALESPERSON Just one?
CUSTOMER Yes, please, and ⁶_____ lemon.
SALESPERSON Um ... no, sorry, we don't have ⁷_____ lemons. But we have ⁸_____ nice bananas.
CUSTOMER But I don't want ⁹_____ bananas. Well, that's all then, thank you.
SALESPERSON OK, so one orange. That's 50 cents, please.
CUSTOMER Oh, no! Sorry, I don't have ¹⁰_____ money.

c Correct one mistake in each sentence.

1 I don't have some tomatoes.
___I don't have any tomatoes.___
2 He doesn't have furnitures.
_____
3 Do you have any moneys?
_____
4 I'd like a onion and a carrot, please.
_____
5 We need a cheese.
_____
6 I don't want some meat.
_____
7 She has long hairs.
_____
8 Do you want any apple?
_____

d ⟫ Now go back to p. 41.

4B Quantifiers: *much, many, a lot of*

a Complete the sentences about the pictures.

1 We have ___a lot of___ apples.

4 We have a _____ lemons.

2 We only have a _____ milk.

5 We don't have _____ butter.

3 We have _____ pasta

6 That's _____ sugar!

b Complete the questions with *much* or *many*.

1 How ___many___ carrots do you want?
2 How _____ money does she have?
3 How _____ bread do we have?
4 How _____ tomatoes do you want?
5 How _____ cheese do we need?
6 How _____ apples do you have?
7 How _____ do postcards cost?
8 How _____ salt do you eat?

c Underline the correct answers.

1 I don't eat *many / much* chocolate.
2 How *many / much* butter do we need?
3 How *many / much* onions do you want?
4 I just need *a few / a little* salt.
5 She doesn't have *many / much* money.
6 He eats *a lot of / a lot* vegetables.
7 Do you drink *many / much* coffee?
8 We have *a few / a little* good restaurants in my town.

d ⟫ Now go back to p. 43.

5A *there is / there are*

We use *there is / there are* to say that something exists in a place.
We often use *there is / there are* with *a/an, some,* and *any*.
We use *some* and *any* with noncount nouns and plural nouns.
We use *some* in affirmative sentences and *any* in negative sentences and questions.

▶ 05.03

	+		−	
Singular	**There's**	a river.	**There isn't** **There's no**	a theater. theater.
Plural	**There are**	some restaurants.	**There aren't** **There are no**	any cafés. cafés.

	Yes/No questions		Short answers	
Singular	**Is there**	a square?	Yes,	**there is.**
			No,	**there isn't.** **there's not.**
Plural	**Are there**	any stores?	Yes,	**there are.**
			No,	**there aren't.**

	Wh- questions		
Count	How **many**	people	**are there?**
Noncount	How **much**	pasta	**is there?**

> 💡 **Tip**
> Use *There's* (NOT ~~There are~~) to talk about a list of singular things:
> **There's a** book, a phone, and a laptop on the table.

5B Possessive pronouns and possessive *'s*

Possessive pronouns

Subject	Possessive adjective	Possessive pronoun ▶ 05.09
I	*my* Those are my shoes.	*mine* Those are **mine**.
you	*your* These are your pens.	**yours** These are **yours**.
he	*his* This is his shirt.	*his* This is **his**.
she	*her* That's her bag.	**hers** That's **hers**.
it	*its* Those are its wheels.	–
we	*our* They're our cats.	**ours** They're **ours**.
they	*their* They aren't their cats.	**theirs** They aren't **theirs**.

▶ 05.10

We use possessive adjectives (e.g., *my, your*) before nouns:
*Is this **your** hat?*
We use possessive pronouns (e.g., *mine, yours*) in the place of a possessive adjective and a noun:
*Is this **yours**?*
We can ask about possession with the word *whose*:
Whose hat is this? / **Whose** is this?

> 💡 **Tip**
> • Be careful with *it's* (= *it is / it has*) and *its* (= possessive adjective).
> • Be careful with *who's* (= *who is / who has*) and *whose*.

Possessive *'s* ▶ 05.11

We add an apostrophe (') + *s* to a singular noun or a name to show possession:
*My sister has a car. It's my sister**'s** car.*
If a plural noun already ends in *-s*, we just add an apostrophe after the *-s*:
*My grandparents have a house. It's my grandparents**'** house.*

Other uses of *'s*
• We also use *'s* as a contraction of *is*:
*He**'s** (= He is) very lucky.*

5A *there is / there are*

a Write sentences about a small town using the information in the chart.

airport	✗		parks	four
cafés	six		schools	not many
stadium	✗		river	✓ (one)
stores	a lot		bridges	two

1 _____There isn't an airport._____
2 _____
3 _____
4 _____
5 _____
6 _____
7 _____
8 _____

b Write questions and short answers about the town, using the information in the chart.

1 _____Is there an airport in the town? No, there isn't._____
2 _____How many_____
3 _____
4 _____
5 _____How many_____
6 _____
7 _____
8 _____How many_____

c Write sentences about the things in the charts in **a** that are true for your town.

1 _____There isn't an airport._____
2 _____There aren't a lot of cafés._____
3 _____
4 _____
5 _____
6 _____
7 _____
8 _____

d ≫ Now go back to p. 51.

5B Possessive pronouns and possessive *'s*

a Complete the sentences with the correct possessive pronouns.

1 It's my pen.

It's _____mine_____.

2 They're her shoes.

They're _____.

3 It's their ball.

It's _____.

4 It's his hat.

It's _____.

5 It's our car.

It's _____.

6 He's your dog.

He's _____.

b Underline the correct words.

1 Excuse me. Is this *your* / *yours*?
2 *Its* / *It's* a very interesting book.
3 *Our* / *Ours* apartment is pretty small.
4 That's my *parent's* / *parents'* room.
5 Don't touch that lamp – it's *my* / *mine*!
6 *Whose* / *Who's* book is this?
7 *Anita's* / *Anitas* house is downtown.
8 What color are *your* / *yours* curtains?

c Underline the *'s* in the conversation. Write *P* (possessive) or *C* (contraction). Then write the full form of the contractions.

ALEXIS Hello. I think I know you. You're in my brother'*s*^P class at school.

NADIA What's your brother's name?

ALEXIS Paul.

NADIA Paul? Yeah, he's in my class. So, you're Paul's sister.

ALEXIS That's right. Well, in fact, Paul has two sisters.

NADIA Oh, yes, I remember. My name's Nadia. What's your name?

ALEXIS I'm Alexis.

NADIA Hi, Alexis. It's nice to meet you.

d ≫ Now go back to p. 53.

6A Simple past: *be*

We use *was/were* to talk about the past.
Was/were are the past forms of *am/is/are*.
We often use past time expressions with *was/were*, e.g., *yesterday*, *last year*, *in 2012*.

▶ 06.05

	+			–		
I / he / she / it	I **was**	at school yesterday.		He **wasn't**	at school yesterday.	
you / we / they	They **were**	at school yesterday.		We **weren't**	at school yesterday.	

	Yes/No questions		Short answers		
I / he / she / it	**Was** she	at school yesterday?	Yes, No,	she **was**. she **wasn't**.	
you / we / they	**Were** you	at school yesterday?	Yes, No,	we **were**. we **weren't**.	

	Wh- questions		
I / he / she / it	Where	**was** he	yesterday?
you / we / they	Where	**were** you	yesterday?

We can also use *there was / there were*:
There was a computer on the table.
There were some chairs in the yard.

My grandparents **were** classmates in high school, but they **weren't** friends then.

6B Simple past: affirmative

Simple past

We use the simple past to describe completed actions in the past.
We often use past time expressions with the simple past, e.g., *yesterday*, *last week*, *when I was a child*.

▶ 06.13

I **arrived** last night.
I **bought** a new car last week.
I often **visited** my grandmother when I was a child.
I sometimes **went** to the theater when I lived in New York.
I **liked** candy a lot when I was young.
I **had** a lot of friends at school.

My parents **bought** me a guitar when I was 12. I **loved** it.

Regular and irregular verbs

Simple past verbs are the same for all persons: *I / you / we / they / he / she / it*.
I worked. **She** worked. **They** worked.
You went. **He** went. **We** went.
Some verbs are regular. We add *-ed* to make the simple past:
work → work**ed**   help → help**ed**
Some verbs are irregular, and you will need to learn their past forms:
meet → **met**   buy → **bought**
There is a list of irregular verbs on p. 129.

SPELLING: regular verbs

most verbs → add *-ed*	start → start**ed** watch → watch**ed**
verb ends in *-e* → add *-d*	live → live**d** die → die**d**
verb ends in consonant + *-y* → change *-y* to *-i* then add *-ed*	try → tr**ied** cry → cr**ied**
verb ends in one vowel (*a, e, i, o, u*) **and one consonant** (*g, n, t,* etc.) → double the consonant and add *-ed*	stop → stop**ped** plan → plan**ned**
never double the consonants *w, x,* or *y* → add *-ed* only	show → show**ed** play → play**ed**

6A Simple past: *he*

a Underline the correct word.

1 I (was) / were on vacation last week.
2 Where *were* / *was* you born?
3 *Wasn't* / *Weren't* there any eggs in the fridge?
4 I *wasn't* / *weren't* at school yesterday; I was sick in bed.
5 There *were* / *was* a lot of people in the store.
6 Why *was* / *were* your friends late?
7 *Was* / *Were* there a laptop on the desk?
8 When *was* / *were* your children born?

b Rewrite the sentences so that they are about the past.

1 My father's a manager. _____My father was a manager._____
2 They aren't friends. _____
3 **A** Is your grandfather rich? **B** No, he isn't.
 _____
4 We're in school together. _____
5 It's a beautiful day. _____
6 My teacher's name's Miss Smith. _____
7 She isn't at home. _____
8 There are 20 people in my class. _____
9 I'm not tired. _____
10 **A** Are you happy? **B** Yes, I am. _____

c Put the words in the correct order to make questions.

1 born / you / where / were ?
 _____Where were you born?_____
2 good / movie / was / the ?
 _____
3 a lot of / there / party / were / people / at / the ?
 _____
4 grandmother's / was / name / your / what ?
 _____
5 school / at / were / yesterday / you ?
 _____
6 was / your hotel / a pool / at / there ?
 _____

d ≫ Now go back to p. 61.

6B Simple past: affirmative

a Write *R* (regular) or *I* (irregular) after each verb. Use the list on page 129 to help you.

1	arrive	11	have
2	become	12	like
3	buy	13	plan
4	come	14	play
5	cook	15	spend
6	decide	16	tell
7	enjoy	17	try
8	find	18	win
9	finish	19	work
10	go	20	write

b Write the simple past forms of the regular verbs in **a**. Be careful with spelling!

1 _____arrived_____
2 _____
3 _____
4 _____
5 _____
6 _____
7 _____
8 _____
9 _____
10 _____

c Complete the sentences with the simple past forms of the verbs in parentheses.

1 When I was a child, we _____had_____ an old computer. (have)
2 They _____ good friends in 1996, and they stayed friends for many years. (become)
3 I lost my phone for about a week, but then I _____ it under my bed! (find)
4 She _____ me an amazing story about Steve Jobs. (tell)
5 It was a very difficult game, but in the end we _____. (win)
6 My uncle was a famous writer. He _____ books for children. (write)
7 I _____ my first computer in 1995. (buy)
8 I _____ for a walk yesterday. (go)
9 When I _____ home, I checked my email. (get)

d Correct one spelling mistake in each sentence.

1 He plaied volleyball when he was young.
 _____played_____
2 I buyed a new bed yesterday, and it cost $450.
 _____
3 I really liket the concert on Saturday.
 _____
4 She eated a piece of cake with her coffee.
 _____
5 They gotten an email about the new class.
 _____
6 We dicide to stay at home last weekend.
 _____

e ≫ Now go back to p. 63.

VOCABULARY FOCUS

1A Countries and nationalities

a ▶ 01.04 Look at the map below. Write the correct number next to each country in the chart. Listen and check.

Country	Nationality	Country	Nationality
A (-ian)		**C (-ish)**	
Argentina	Argentin**ian**	Ireland	Ir**ish**
Australia	Austral**ian**	Poland	Pol**ish**
Canada	Canad**ian**	Turkey	Turk**ish**
Colombia	Colomb**ian**	(the) UK	Brit**ish**
Ecuador	Ecuador**ian**	Britain	Brit**ish**
Iran	Iran**ian**	**D (-ese)**	
Italy	Ital**ian**	China	Chinese
Nigeria	Niger**ian**	Japan	Japanese
Russia	Russ**ian**	**E (-i)**	
		Pakistan	Pakistan**i**
B (-an)		**F (other)**	
Mexico	Mexic**an**	New Zealand	(a) New Zealander
South Africa	South Afric**an**	Saudi Arabia	Saudi
(the) U.S.	Americ**an**		

b 💬 Talk about five countries you want to visit.

> I'd like to visit China because I want to see the Great Wall of China.

c Match the parts of the world 1–6 with a–f on the map.

1 North America
2 Asia
3 Central and South America
4 Africa
5 Europe
6 Oceania

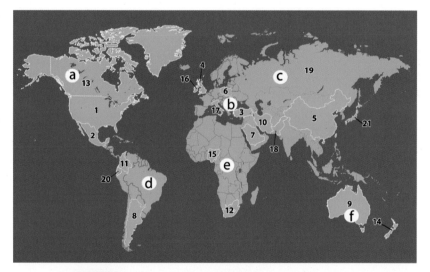

d 💬 Underline the different country in each group below. Say why.

1 France, Italy, Greece, Poland, China, Germany, Ireland
2 Turkey, Saudi Arabia, Brazil, Iran
3 the U.S., Russia, the UK, Australia, Canada
4 Argentina, Mexico, Colombia, Spain

e Look at groups A–F in **a**. Match each nationality below to a group.

1 Brazilian
2 Spanish
3 Mexican
4 Indian
5 Japanese
6 French

f ▶ 01.05 **Pronunciation** Listen to the nationalities in the chart. <u>Underline</u> the stressed syllable in each word.

A	2 syllables	Brit|ish, Chi|nese, Tur|kish
B	3 syllables	Mex|i|can, Ja|pa|nese, Bra|zil|ian
C	4 syllables	Ca|na|di|an, Pa|ki|sta|ni

g ▶ 01.05 Look at the nationalities in **f** again and answer the questions. Listen again and check.

1 In A, which word has a different stress pattern?
2 In B and in C, do the words have the same or a different stress pattern?

h 💬 Student A: choose a new country and a nationality. Tell your partner the part of the world. Then answer his/her questions. Student B: ask questions to guess your partner's new country and nationality. Change roles and repeat.

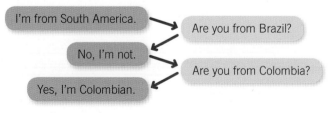

> I'm from South America.
> Are you from Brazil?
> No, I'm not.
> Are you from Colombia?
> Yes, I'm Colombian.

i ⟫ Now go back to p. 11.

1B Adjectives

a ▶ 01.08 Listen to these sentences. Do the adjectives in **bold** mean "very good" or "not very good"?

1 This wet and cold weather is **terrible**.
2 I like our new teacher – she's **wonderful**.
3 My new phone does so many great things – it's **amazing**.
4 This color isn't very nice – it's **awful**.

b ▶ 01.09 Listen to these sentences. Make pairs of opposites with the adjectives in **bold**.

1 My computer's pretty **old** now. I need to buy a new one.
2 I don't think he has much money – he's **poor**.
3 Their new house is finished now, and it's very **modern**.
4 He buys anything he wants, so I think he's **rich**.

c Think of things you have. Take notes. Do you have anything that's … ?

- wonderful
- amazing
- terrible
- awful
- old
- modern

d 💬 Tell a partner about your things using your notes in **c**.

e ⟫ Now go back to p. 13.

2A Jobs

a ▶ 02.02 Match the jobs in the box with pictures 1–9. Listen and check. Listen again and repeat.

| businessman | businesswoman | receptionist | manager | chef | actor |
| tour guide | farmer | server | mechanic | | |

b Look at the jobs on page 21 and in **a**. Read the sentences and write the correct job.

a I work in a hospital and take care of people.
b I work outside and enjoy showing people my beautiful city.
c I sometimes work in a theater, and I sometimes make movies.
d I drive people from one place to another.
e I work in a kitchen and cook amazing food.
f I help people if they have a problem with their teeth.
g I help people if they have a problem with their car.
h I fly people from one country to another.
i I am the first person people meet when they come to our hotel.
j I work outside in the country.

c 💬 Talk about three jobs you would like to do and three jobs you wouldn't like to do. Say why.

d ⟫ Now go back to p. 21.

NUMBERS

2B Time

a ▶️02.08 Match the sentences (1–9) with the times (a–i). Listen and check.

1. It's (a) quarter after four. *or* It's four fifteen.
2. It's four thirty. *or* It's half past four.
3. It's (a) quarter to five. *or* It's four forty-five.
4. It's twenty after four. *or* It's four twenty.
5. It's ten to five. *or* It's four fifty.
6. It's five after four. *or* It's four oh five.
7. It's twenty-five to five. *or* It's four thirty-five.
8. It's four minutes to five. *or* It's four fifty-six.
9. It's seven minutes after four. *or* It's four oh seven.

b Write down five different times in numbers. Ask your partner to say your times.

c ≫ Now go back to p. 23.

PLACES

5A Places in a city

a ▶️05.01 Match the places in the box with pictures 1–6. There are three extra words. Listen and check.

post office ☐   fitness center ☐   theater ☐   police station ☐   concert hall ☐   stadium ☐   bridge ☐   park ☐   hotel ☐

b Match the definitions with the places in **a** and on page 51.

a. You go there to watch a sports game.
b. This is a nice place to sit with trees and grass and flowers.
c. When you want to send a postcard, you go to this place.
d. You walk on this from one side of a river to the other side.
e. You can see a play in this place.
f. If someone steals from you, you go to this place.
g. This is an open area in the center of a town.
h. You can listen to classical music in this place.
i. When you want to do some exercise, you go to this place.

c ▶️05.02 **Pronunciation** Listen to the words. Two of the sounds in **bold** are produced with extra air. Which ones? Listen again and repeat.

building   **b**ridge   **p**ark   **p**ost office

d 💬 In pairs ask and answer the questions.

1. Which of the places in **b** does / doesn't your city have?
2. Which does / doesn't your city need?

e ≫ Now go back to p. 51.

VERBS

3A Common verbs

a ▶03.06 Match 1–7 with a–g. Listen and check.

1 How much is the coffee?
2 Do you drink coffee in the morning?
3 Can I **help** you paint the kitchen?
4 Where's your passport?
5 Do you know where I can **buy** an English newspaper?
6 The movie starts at 8:15, so let's **meet** outside the movie theater at 8:00.
7 Do you want to go for a walk this evening?

a I think they **sell** them at the store in the subway station.
b It's very cheap. It only **costs** $1 a cup.
c No, I just want to **stay** at home and watch TV.
d OK. I'll **try** to be on time, but I don't leave work until 7:30.
e Yes, please! But I can't **decide** what color: blue or green.
f Sometimes, but I **prefer** tea.
g I don't know. I can't **find** it. It isn't in my bag.

b ▶03.07 **Pronunciation** Listen to the sounds in **bold** in these words and answer the questions. Listen again and repeat.

b**uy** f**i**nd d**e**cide tr**y** st**a**y

1 Which word has a different sound?
2 Are the two different sounds long or short?

c In pairs ask and answer the questions.

1 What do you like to drink in the morning?
2 Think of a small store near your home. What do they sell? What do you buy there?
3 How much do these things cost in your country?
   a an ice cream cone
   b a cup of coffee
   c a loaf of bread
4 You decide to meet friends in town. Where do you meet?
5 Where do you usually stay on vacation?

d ≫ Now go back to p. 31.

6B Simple past irregular verbs

a ▶06.15 Match the simple past forms in the box with 1–11. Listen and check.

brought	won	lost	found	did	cut
read	thought	sold	became	gave	

1 do
2 read
3 give
4 think
5 bring
6 win
7 lose
8 find
9 become
10 cut
11 sell

b ▶06.16 **Pronunciation** Listen to these sentences. Do the letters in **bold** sound the same or different? Why?

• I **rea**d a newspaper every day.
• I **rea**d a wonderful book last month.

c ▶06.17 Read the story and underline the correct verbs. Listen and check.

How I [1]*won / lost* the lottery

One day, I went into town and [2]*did / made* some shopping. Then, on the way home, I [3]*brought / bought* a lottery ticket from a convenience store by the bus stop. It had the number of my birthday: 072493. A very nice woman [4]*spent / sold* it to me. When she [5]*gave / took* it to me, she smiled and said, "Good luck. I hope you win." I smiled back. A few days later, I looked online and [6]*gave / read* the winning number: 2-4-7 ... That was the moment I [7]*decided / found out*. My life completely changed and I [8]*became / came* rich. I immediately [9]*thought / told* of the woman in the convenience store. I [10]*cost / cut* some fresh flowers from my garden and went back to the store to give them to her. "Is the woman who was here on Saturday in today?" I asked. "I have some flowers for her." But she wasn't there, and I never saw her again.

d 💬 Cover the text in **c** and practice telling the story from the pictures. Read it again to check.

e ≫ Now go back to p. 63.

6A Years and dates

a ▶06.09 Put the months in the correct order. Listen and check. Listen again and repeat.

June	September	April	November
January	August	February	December
May	March	October	July

b ▶06.10 Complete the sentences with *in* or *on*. Listen and check.

1 We were in Australia _____ 2019.
2 My birthday's _____ June nineteenth.
3 Our next day off from school is _____ May.

c Correct the dates. Then write them in number form.

                                              twelfth
1 The next meeting's on April ~~twelve~~. April 12th
2 Our party's on Saturday, February twenty-one.
3 We were in Canada in twenty oh seven.
4 Next Saturday's July seven.
5 I was in college until one thousand nine hundred and ninety-eight.
6 I'd like to reserve a single room for December two.

d Think of two people in your family and two friends. Write down their names.

e 💬 Tell a partner the birthdays of the four people. Can they match the birthdays with the names?

f ≫ Now go back to p. 61.

FOOD AND CONTAINERS

4A Food

a ▶ 04.03 Match pictures 1–10 with definitions a–j. Listen and check.

1 garlic   2 salad   3 burger   4 melon   5 cereal   6 yogurt   7 jam

8 soda   9 chips   10 cookie

a It's sweet. People bake it in the oven and eat it for a snack or dessert.
b It's a large fruit which grows in hot countries. It's red, orange, or green.
c It's a quick, cheap meal: meat and salad inside bread, sometimes with cheese.
d It's uncooked vegetables mixed together that you can have with a meal. It's good for you!
e It's like onion and you can use it for cooking.
f It's made from milk. People often have it for breakfast.
g It's sweet and it's made from fruit. You can put it on bread.
h They're made from potatoes and usually come in small bags. They aren't very good for you!
i It's a drink. It's fizzy, sweet, and brown.
j Many people eat it for breakfast with milk.

b ▶ 04.04 **Pronunciation** Listen to the sounds in **bold** in these words. Listen again and repeat.

/k/ **c**ookie   **c**an   **c**arrot
/g/ **g**arlic   bur**g**er   yo**g**urt

c ▶ 04.05 Which words do you hear, a or b?

1 a could b good   **3** a class b glass
2 a cold   b gold   **4** a back   b bag

d 💬🔊 Say a word from **c** for your partner to point to.

e Complete the sentences. Use words from **a** and page 41.

1 What kind of meat do you want; c_____n, s_____k, or l_____b?
2 Let's have a s_____d. We have tomatoes, o_____ns, c_____ts, green b_____ns, and m_____ms.
3 My wife has c_____l and milk for breakfast, but I like y_____t with fruit and then a piece of bread with butter and j_____m.
4 We have a lot of fruit: apples, p_____rs, g_____pes, and a m_____n.
5 Of course he's not fit. He always eats c_____ps and drinks s_____a between meals.

f 💬🔊 Look at all the words in **a** and **e**. Talk about:

- things you eat or drink almost every day
- things you eat or drink at least once a week
- things you don't often eat or drink
- things you never eat or drink

g ⟫ Now go back to p. 41.

4B Containers

a Match phrases 1–6 with pictures a–f below.

1 a **jar** of honey
2 a **bag** of potatoes
3 a **can** of tomatoes
4 a **bottle** of water
5 a **bar** of chocolate
6 a **package** of cookies

b ▶ 04.11 **Pronunciation** Listen to the phrases in **a**. Which words are stressed? Listen again and repeat.

1 the nouns   3 the preposition *of*
2 the article *a*

c Change the words in italics using phrases in **a**. Is more than one answer possible?

> Yesterday I went shopping and bought ¹*some oil,* ²*some jam,* ³*some spaghetti,* ⁴*some chocolate,* ⁵*some tuna,* and ⁶*some apples.*

1 _a bottle of oil_   4 _____
2 _____   5 _____
3 _____   6 _____

d 💬🔊 Write a shopping list. Use the words in **a** to help you. Tell a partner.

e ⟫ Now go back to p. 43.

Acknowledgments

The authors and publishers acknowledge the following sources of copyright material and are grateful for the permissions granted. While every effort has been made, it has not always been possible to identify the sources of all the material used, or to trace all copyright holders. If any omissions are brought to our notice, we will be happy to include the appropriate acknowledgments on reprinting and in the next update to the digital edition, as applicable.

Key:
U = Unit, CL = Classroom Language, C = Communication Plus, V = Vocabulary Focus

Text
U2: We are grateful to Gabriella Scampone for granting us permission to write the text about her.

Photographs
All the photographs are sourced from Getty Images.
Front cover photography by Franz Aberham/Photolibrary/Getty Images Plus/ Getty Images; **CL:** Dragonimages/iStock/Getty Images Plus; Skynesher/E+; Drazen_/E+; Photoalto/Dinoco Greco; Hjalmeidaistock/Getty Images Plus; Studiocasper/E+; Akepong Srichaichana/Eyeem; Alesveluscek/E+; Nattawut Lakjit/Eyeem; Blackred/E+; Daydreamsgirl/iStock/Getty Images Plus; Adha Ghazali/Eyeem; Tony Robins/Photolibrary/Getty Images Plus; **U1:** Piola666/E+; Africaimages/E+; Michael Blann/Stone/Getty Images Plus; Alex Livesey/Getty Images Sport; Pierre-Philippe Marcou/Afp; James D. Morgan/Getty Images Sport; Patrik Stollarz/Afp; Franckreporter/iStock/Getty Images Plus; Shy Al Britanni/Arabianeye; Filippobacci/E+; Caiaimage; Tetra Images; Westend61; Juanmonino/E+; Morsa Images/Digitalvision; Sturti/E+; Eloi_Omella/E+; **U2:** David Madison/Photographer'S Choice RF; Bluebarronphoto/iStock/Getty Images Plus; Alexander Yates/Moment Open; Piotrsurowiec/iStock Editorial/Getty Images Plus; Caiaimage; Hill Street Studios/Digitalvision; Monkeybusinessimages/ iStock/Getty Images Plus; Image Source/Digitalvision; Antonioguillem/iStock/ Getty Images Plus; Fstop123/E+; Shironosov/iStock/Getty Images Plus; SDI Productions/E+; Lightfieldstudios/iStock/Getty Images Plus; Argument/iStock/ Getty Images Plus; Zephyr18/iStock/Getty Images Plus; Jacoblund/iStock/ Getty Images Plus; Westend61; Peopleimages/E+; Сергей Марков/iStock/ Getty Images Plus; Jlgutierrez/E+; Anabgd/iStock/Getty Images Plus; Chevanon Wonganuchitmetha/Eyeem; Antonio_Diaz/iStock/Getty Images Plus; Klaus Vedfelt/Digitalvision; Tom Merton/Ojo Images; Drazen_/E+; JohnnyGreig/E+; Flashpop/Digitalvision; Emirmemedovski/E+; Yacobchuk/iStock/Getty Images Plus; Andresr/E+; **U3:** Fangxianuo/E+; Maskot; Chairman Ting Creative, Chairmanting.Com/Moment/Getty Images Plus; Luis Alvarez/Digitalvision; Drazen_/E+; Hero Images; Dimitri Otis/Photographer'S Choice/Getty Images Plus; Eri Morita/The Image Bank/Getty Images Plus; Monkeybusinessimages/ iStock/Gett; Olix Wirtinger/Corbis/VCG/Getty Images Plus; Johnnygreig/E+; Tim Robberts/Taxi/Getty Images Plus; Yuri_Arcurs/E+; Grinvalds/iStock/Getty Images Plus; Roulier/Turiot; Gradyreese/E+; Iryna Kurilovych/iStock/Getty Images Plus; **U4:** Ippei Naoi/Moment; Craig Ferguson/Lightrocket; Thomas Barwick/Digitalvision; Adam Hester/Photolibrary/Getty Images Plus; John Lamparski/Wireimage; Todd Wright; Scaliger/iStock/Getty Images Plus; Mint Images; Hispanolistic/E+; Manuta/iStock/Getty Images Plus; Westend61; Lori Andrews/Moment; Tony Robins/Photolibrary/Getty Images Plus; Eric Audras/ Onoky; Maskot; Allen Simon/Digitalvision; **U5:** Franckreporter/E+; Mlgxyz/ Moment; Johnny Haglund/Lonely Planet Images/Getty Images Plus; Luis Emilio Villegas Amador/Eyeem; Firmafotografen/iStock/Getty Images Plus; Bonetta/ iStock/Getty Images Plus; Donnichols/iStock/Getty Images Plus; Nerthuz/ iStock/Getty Images Plus; David Crunelle/Eyeem; Matthewjean-Louis/iStock/ Getty Images Plus; S-Cphoto/iStock/Getty Images Plus; Phototropic/iStock/ Getty Images Plus; Jaswinder Singh/iStock/Getty Images Plus; Rosshelen/ iStock/Getty Images Plus; Hraun/E+; Feifei Cui-Paoluzzo/Moment; Juststock/ iStock/Getty Images Plus; Innocenti/Cultura; Dglimages/iStock/Getty Images Plus; JGI; Jhorrocks/E+; D3Sign/Moment; Yacobchuk/iStock/Getty Images Plus; Caiaimage; **U6:** Aldomurillo/E+; Momo Productions/Digitalvision; Morsa Images/ Digitalvision; Dean Mitchell/iStock/Getty Images Plus; Caiaimage; Westend61; Juanmonino/E+; Peopleimages/E+; Cavan Images; Ana Francisconi/Eyeem; Jose Luis Pelaez Inc/Digitalvision; Juvenal Makoszay/Eyeem; George Marks/Retrofile RF; Justin Sullivan/Getty Images News; David Pu'U/Corbis Documentary/Getty Images Plus; Tom Munnecke/Hulton Archive; Andresr/E+; Delmaine Donson/ E+; Neustockimages/E+; Jose A. Bernat Bacete/Moment; Starcevic/iStock/Getty Images Plus.

The following images are sourced from other Sourced/libraries.

U2: © Gabriella Scampone and © Everglades Holiday Park: photograph reproduced with kind permission of Gabriella Scampone; **U5:** © Reed Young.

Commissioned photography by Gareth Boden.

Illustrations by QBS Learning; Adrian Barclay; Mark Bird; Mark Duffin; John Goodwin; KJA Artists; Dusan Lakicevic; Jerome Mireault; Gavin Reece; Martin Sanders; David Semple; Sean Sims; Marie-Eve Tremblay; Gary Venn; Roger Penwill.

Typeset by QBS Learning.

Audio by John Marshall Media.

Corpus Development of this publication has made use of the Cambridge English Corpus(CEC). The CEC is a computer database of contemporary spoken and written English, which currently stands at over one billion words. It includes British English, American English and other varieties of English. It also includes the Cambridge Learner Corpus, developed in collaboration with the University of Cambridge ESOL Examinations. Cambridge University Press has built up the CEC to provide evidence about language use that helps us to produce better language teaching materials.

English Profile This product is informed by English Vocabulary Profile, built as part of English Profile, a collaborative program designed to enhance the learning, teaching and assessment of English worldwide. Its main funding partners are Cambridge University Press and Cambridge Assessment English and its aim is to create a "profile" for English, linked to the Common European Framework of Reference for Languages (CEFR). English Profile outcomes, such as the English Vocabulary Profile, will provide detailed information about the language that learners can be expected to demonstrate at each CEFR level, offering a clear benchmark for learners' proficiency. For more information, please visit www.englishprofile.org.

CALD The Cambridge Advanced Learner's Dictionary is the world's most widely used dictionary for learners of English. Including all the words and phrases that learners are likely to come across, it also has easy-to-understand definitions and example sentences to show how the word is used in context. The Cambridge Advanced Learner's Dictionary is available online at dictionary.cambridge.org.

Shaftesbury Road, Cambridge CB2 8EA, United Kingdom

One Liberty Plaza, 20th Floor, New York, NY 10006, USA

477 Williamstown Road, Port Melbourne, VIC 3207, Australia

314–321, 3rd Floor, Plot 3, Splendor Forum, Jasola District Centre, New Delhi – 110025, India

103 Penang Road, #05-06/07, Visioncrest Commercial, Singapore 238467

Cambridge University Press & Assessment is a department of the University of Cambridge.

We share the University's mission to contribute to society through the pursuit of education, learning and research at the highest international levels of excellence.

www.cambridge.org
Information on this title: www.cambridge.org/9781108862448

First published 2022

20 19 18 17 16 15 14 13 12 11 10 9 8 7

Printed in Poland by Opolgraf

A catalogue record for this publication is available from the British Library

ISBN 978-1-108-81751-6 Elementary Student's Book with eBook
ISBN 978-1-108-79716-0 Elementary Student's Book A with eBook
ISBN 978-1-108-79717-7 Elementary Student's Book B with eBook
ISBN 978-1-108-85046-9 Elementary Student's Book with Digital Pack
ISBN 978-1-108-86244-8 Elementary Student's Book A with Digital Pack
ISBN 978-1-108-86247-9 Elementary Student's Book B with Digital Pack
ISBN 978-1-108-81755-4 Elementary Workbook with Answers
ISBN 978-1-108-81756-1 Elementary Workbook A with Answers
ISBN 978-1-108-81757-8 Elementary Workbook B with Answers
ISBN 978-1-108-81758-5 Elementary Workbook without Answers
ISBN 978-1-108-81759-2 Elementary Workbook A without Answers
ISBN 978-1-108-81760-8 Elementary Workbook B without Answers
ISBN 978-1-108-81761-5 Elementary Full Contact with eBook
ISBN 978-1-108-81762-2 Elementary Full Contact A with eBook
ISBN 978-1-108-81763-9 Elementary Full Contact B with eBook
ISBN 978-1-108-85051-3 Elementary Full Contact with Digital Pack
ISBN 978-1-108-85054-4 Elementary Full Contact A with Digital Pack
ISBN 978-1-108-86243-1 Elementary Full Contact B with Digital Pack
ISBN 978-1-108-79719-1 Elementary Teacher's Book with Digital Pack
ISBN 978-1-108-79723-8 Elementary Presentation Plus

Additional resources for this publication at www.cambridge.org/americanempower

This page is intentionally left blank.

This page is intentionally left blank.

This page is intentionally left blank.

This page is intentionally left blank.

This page is intentionally left blank.

This page is intentionally left blank.